PENGUIN BOOKS

THE RUSH FOR SECOND PLACE

William Gaddis (1922–1998) was twice awarded the National Book Award, for his novels *J R* and *A Frolic of His Own*. His other novels were *The Recognitions*, *Carpenter's Gothic*, and *Agapē Agape*. He was a member of the American Academy of Arts and Letters and the recipient of a MacArthur Prize.

Joseph Tabbi is the author of *Cognitive Fictions*, a comprehensive look at the effect of new technologies on contemporary fiction, and the founding editor of *ebr*, the electronic book review. He was the first scholar to be given access to the Gaddis archives in the summer of 2001. Tabbi conducts research in American literature and new media writing at the University of Illinois at Chicago.

William Gaddis

THE RUSH FOR SECOND PLACE

Essays and Occasional Writings

EDITED WITH HEADNOTES
AND AN
INTRODUCTION BY JOSEPH TABBI

PENGUIN BOOKS

PENGUIN BOOKS
Published by the Penguin Group
Penguin Putnam Inc., 375 Hudson Street,
New York, New York 10014, U.S.A.
Penguin Books Ltd, 80 Strand,
London WC2R 0RL, England
Penguin Books Australia Ltd, 250 Camberwell Road,
Camberwell, Victoria 3124, Australia
Penguin Books Canada Ltd, 10 Alcorn Avenue,
Toronto, Ontario, Canada M4V 3B2
Penguin Books India (P) Ltd, 11 Community Centre,
Panchsheel Park, New Delhi – 110 017, India
Penguin Books (N.Z.) Ltd, Cnr Rosedale and Airborne Roads,
Albany, Auckland, New Zealand
Penguin Books (South Africa) (Pty) Ltd, 24 Sturdee Avenue,
Rosebank, Johannesburg 2196, South Africa

Penguin Books Ltd, Registered Offices:
Harmondsworth, Middlesex, England

First published in Penguin Books 2002

"Stop Player. Joke No. 4" first appeared in *The Atlantic Monthly*; "In the Zone"
in *The New York Times*; "The Rush for Second Place" in *Harper's*; "J R Up to Date"
(in different form), "An Instinct for the Dangerous Wife," and "Erewhon and the
Contract with America" in *The New York Times Book Review*; "Old Foes with
New Faces" in *The Yale Review*; "J. Danforth Quayle" in Esquire; and tributes
to Dostoevski and Mothers in *Frankfurter Allgemenine Zeitung*.

ISBN 0 14 20.0238 0
CIP data available
ISBN 978-0-142-00238-4 (international)

Set in Aldus
Designed by M. Paul

146434929

Contents

INTRODUCTION

> NOTICE: Persons attempting to find a motive in this narrative
> will be prosecuted; persons attempting to find a moral in it will
> be banished; persons attempting to find a plot in it will be shot.
> By order of the author.
>
> —Mark Twain

WILLIAM GADDIS'S EARLY TREATMENT by unprepared reviewers is well known; perhaps less known is the fact that he wrote a good deal of criticism himself—more than Thomas Pynchon so far, more than Don DeLillo or David Markson, and much that approaches the best critical writing by William Gass, Harry Mathews, Joseph McElroy, or Robert Coover. Criticism as a way of commingling with the work of other writers was not congenial to him, and apart from one front-page review of Saul Bellow's novel *More Die of Heartbreak* (for which he wildly *over*prepared, as though he were getting ready to do a dissertation), he published very few commentaries on the work of his contemporaries. Still less was he inclined to comment on his own work or point the way for other commentators. The handwritten "notices" he left here and there throughout his papers were posted, evidently, only for posterity.

Gaddis did not depreciate the critical faculty; on the contrary, he widened the boundaries of fiction to include criticism. His novels are critical in the sense that each one creates out of past literatures and current languages a separate standard for itself: "Disciplined recognitions," as Wyatt Gwyon says in *The Recognitions*. The nonfiction project that overwhelms Jack Gibbs in *J R* is quarried from a book-length essay Gaddis himself had worked on throughout the sixties: "a social history of mechanization and the arts" that brings insights from cybernetics and classical political theory to bear on the artist's marginal position in society. Gaddis's final fiction, *Agapē Agape*, continues this critical engagement with technology in relation to the arts, even as his earliest, unpublished parodies—another form of criticism—might portray Kit Marlowe's death at the hands of his anthologists and commercial handlers.[1] In *Carpenter's Gothic*, secular liberalism's argument with Christian fundamentalism plays itself out in a devil's debate, with McCandless defending his *roman à clef* against Lester's accusation that the book is "mean and empty like everybody in it." And what is all the legal hairsplitting over Oscar's play in *A Frolic of His Own*, if not a continuation of Gaddis's lifelong obsession with issues of copyright, plagiarism, and intellectual ownership? The novel as a generic form was all things to Gaddis; not least, it was a medium for criticism.

Although Gaddis refused to follow after his books with explanations, he would on occasion elaborate themes from the novels in pieces written for radio, monthly magazines, award ceremonies, university colloquia, and one scholarly journal; there even exist film scripts, treatments, and executive speeches from the period when he made a living writing for small businesses and transnational corporations. As "disciplined recognitions," the essays and occasional writings are, in fact, largely patchworks of quotations, not all of them literary—and like his fiction they may be read (or, more properly, *listened to*) as a score for many voices, from every class and corner of American life. Not all of the pieces are first-rate. Some were never published and a few remain in the rough, as notes for a verbal presentation. In one of the speeches, upon receiving his second National Book Award in 1995, Gaddis mentions the decree by Justice Oliver Wendell Holmes Jr. that "all his papers would be burned. He said, simply, I want to be known by the finished product"—the opinions and dissents—"how I got there is no one else's business." Gaddis felt that way, too. Still, we have the archive, and as a guide through it we have documents that Gaddis entrusted to literary agents and project directors, occasional live audiences, librarians, and future editors and translators. Taken together, the essays, working papers, and project descriptions create a sense of the environment in which Gaddis worked and they reveal, for the first time, continuities between the novels and every form of critical writing that he undertook during his varied professional life.

Literary Imagination and the Imagination of the State

Gaddis's account of the player piano project—which he revived and set aside periodically but never wholly dropped—is perhaps the most lucid statement of what he *would* accomplish, over time, in his novels: "a satirical celebration of the conquest of technology and of the place of art and the artist in a technological democracy." In the archive, boxed together with the essay drafts are pages upon pages of notes that Gaddis assembled over the period of half a century on the history of the player piano. These are the same notes, evidently, that Jack Gibbs in *J R* and "the man in the bed" in the late fiction *Agapē Agape* despaired of ever organizing and turning into a finished work. Each of these protagonists, and Oscar Crease immobilized amid boxes of "evidence" for his original play in *A Frolic of His Own*, struggles against time and entropy and an increasingly mediated culture that largely succeeded, in Gaddis's lifetime, in redefining the creative artist as a performer. Not content merely to document the artist's own rush to obsolescence, Gaddis sought its reasons in history, philosophy, and social theory. In the short essay from the early sixties "Agapē Agape," published here for the first time, he proposed that "the frail human element" (and its surprising ability to surpass itself) was being subordinated to programmatic management in every sphere of life—Spencer's survivalist ethics, Freud's psychology, Taylor's work, Dewey's facts, William James's things, Thorndike's intelligence, and the entire system of control and communication facilitated by the emerging science of cybernetics. Gaddis's uniqueness, and one source of his perceived difficulty, is nothing other than his determination to grapple with these thoroughly transforming conditions (which also transformed realism in fiction, or should have).

Writing for a public that had little time for his infinitely accurate, infinitely detailed representations, Gaddis understood the relative weakness of literary fiction in comparison with the state's collective imagination of itself. He knew how the writer's own attempts to embrace reality play against powerful unrealities in the administered world. "How Does the State Imagine?," his speech to the International PEN Congress, names in its title Gaddis's great theme: that America is itself a "grand fiction" second only to religion, exacting not only taxes from its people but—more crucially—a continuing faith in its own existence, or at least the suspension of disbelief. Relentless though Gaddis may have been as a satirist, he did not create an alternative to state power merely "through calling attention to inequities and abuses, hypocrisies and patent frauds, self-deceiving attitudes and self-defeating policies." His fiction is not *opposed* to religion or the state. His convictions, though forcefully stated, are not the convictions of competing fundamentalisms whose concern is only with winning. Rather, his work tries to discover what individual life can and should be in the midst of collective life and competing fictions. To place second in the competition is not the worst outcome for a writer, who sometimes does better by standing aside and watching the operations of power, appropriating its language, recycling its massive waste products, and reading significance in what has been left behind by the rush of progress. This is how the writer creates a critical space for him- or herself, for the "responsible intelligence" needed to conduct an individual life under regimes of information, unreality, and bureaucratic domination.

Although Gaddis worked within the American grain and centered himself on the classics of literature, philosophy, and the arts, these critical writings reveal a mind that participated fully in the currents of contemporary thought. He was an eclectic writer and a conscientious collector who habitually updated old themes and ancient conundra with clippings from the morning paper. And though he was known for his reticence, he was, like Cicero, on occasion capable of donning a toga and speaking out, if not with a senator's dignity then in the voice of a grown-up J R called to witness at a congressional hearing on the federal budget (see "*J R* Up to Date"). As a high-standing citizen of the Republic of Letters, he could appreciate a peer or rediscover a past author with whom he felt affinities (not least the fellowship of the unjustly neglected). When recognition came, overdue and largely from abroad, he would answer his followers with public missives that are perspicuous about past literary lives even as they reveal an extraordinary ability to nurse a grudge through the decades, to keep alive the outrage that energized his work to the end.

Like Samuel Butler, the subject of his most sustained appreciation, Gaddis would claim that he wrote so that he would have something to read when he was old.

He always wrote for the long term, less a Cicero finally than a modern Horace (who counseled writers never to publish until a manuscript had been set aside for at least ten years). Gaddis's lifelong project on mechanization and the arts, presented through an outdated, homespun industry—the manufacture of paper piano rolls in the United States—now appears prescient and entirely topical. For Gaddis knew what current historians and artists have only begun to discover: that the digital age was anticipated by the arts—in fact no less than imagination. "Music did it," says a programmer in Richard Powers's novel *Plowing the Dark* (2000): "Hollerith got his idea for the punched data card from the player piano. From the Jacquard tapestry loom." That is one reason why the player piano held such a fascination for Gaddis: its automatic operation, like a "shuttle weaving without a hand to guide it," perfectly demonstrated the incommensurability of technology's programmable ends (and accumulating uncontrolled side effects) and his own more forthright immersion in uncertainty, unpredictability, and the environment of failure that conditions any local success achieved in art.

There is an ineradicable emptiness at the heart of technological progress: zeroes punched in rolling paper, the absence—a literal "gap"—at the heart of agapē, the foundationless ideal and necessity of fraternal love. Gaddis worked out the entire idea complex for *Agapē Agape* on his own, through broad cultural observations and wholly literary means, over years of patient composition, recomposition, dismantling, and renewed observation. (Even his writing methods took uncertainty and the passage of time into account so as to allow organizing principles to emerge from the materials rather than be imposed on them. Gaddis would arrange snippets of dialogue, quotations, and other narrative elements on pages laid out on a large table and pinned to the wall; then he would rearrange and rework the whole, trying for the right flow so that each page might go through six or eight revisions before he ever arrived at a "first draft.") He did not rely on the art world or current theory for his insights, although he would generally welcome confirmations as they arrived seemingly daily and from every quarter:

NEW (for me) WORD: APORIA (from a Gertrude Himmelfarb review)

"difference, discontinuity, disparity, contradiction, discord, ambiguity, irony, paradox, perversity, opacity, obscurity, anarchy, chaos"

LONG LIVE![2]

Literally, an "impassable path." The term, favored in contemporary critical theory, is right for an author who felt a need, with every new project, to create a new set of obstacles or narrative problems that he could then overcome. A compendium of forgeries, past and persisting, is the background to multiple quests for truth in his first novel, *The Recognitions*. His next book, *J R*, would be written predominantly in dialogue and with no chapter breaks. A variation on the Harlequin romance, *Carpenter's Gothic* came to be written in the same conversational mode, but this time moving back and forth in time, observing the classical unity of place and employing all of the clichés and lurid turns of gothic fiction. The plot of *A Frolic of His Own* is made to advance through sequences written in the form of a judicial opinion or a deposition or a legal briefing. What blocks the literary imagination is precisely what stimulated Gaddis to further creativity. By setting himself challenges equal to the world's own constraints and resistances, he could discover what freedom and autonomy might be possible, in the here and now, for an individual life and talent.

Johan Huizinga, a favorite philosopher of Gaddis's, has noted that the Greeks were fond of "the *aporia* as a parlour-game, i.e., the propounding of questions impossible to answer conclusively."[3] This disposition toward ambiguity and uncertainty, play rather than purity in the use of language, of course distinguishes the critical mind and critical discourse from fundamentalist thought ("clothed in revealed religion," as Gaddis says in the radio essay on Dostoevski). Students in the arts and humanities learn to approach a text critically by making comparisons and exploring ambiguities. A fundamentalist, by contrast, reads a text single-mindedly, as a source of facts only: the "scientifically" revealed objective text that leaves no room for interpretation. But the world remains stubbornly multiple for all that, as one lexicon breeds its opposite among true believers who counter the abstract with the concrete, the pluralistic with the monistic, the deductive with the inductive, the historical, skeptical, and deferential with the ahistorical, solemn, and authoritarian. Any neoconservative concept can always find its liberal counterpart—Gertrude Himmelfarb can always be countered with Arthur Schlessinger Jr.—

but Gaddis, by setting these and other old foes against one another in his key essay on religion, "Old Foes with New Faces," avoids taking sides in ageless religious battles and never-ending "culture wars." A critical mind cannot simply choose between uncertainty and truth, relativism and absolutism, Protestant individualism and Catholic authoritarianism. These choices Gaddis leaves to the fundamentalists of either side.

When asked about the turn to a radical empiricism, in *J R*, twenty years after the passionate and parodied religion in *The Recognitions*, Gaddis responded that at a certain point in his adult life the religion just "went away." When he returned to the subject in *Carpenter's Gothic*, his concern was not with the truth content of a religious movement but with "more of a secular, which is to say political, threat" from the newly organized Christian right.[4] The American state, by virtue of its radical separation from a supposedly depoliticized religion, has consistently underestimated the strength of religiously motivated activism. Gaddis never made that mistake. The nexus between organized religion, vast monetary networks, and a global economy dependent on inexpensive oil and natural resources has long been a primary topic of investigation for Gaddis. After considering his reflections on revealed religion, readers might want to look again at *Carpenter's Gothic* and its account of the transactions, both human and material, between the Reverend Ude, a U.S. senator, McCandless the geologist, and the great African rift in its background, where "it all began." Gaddis's heart of darkness is not, like Joseph Conrad's, racially motivated; it is instead a place where debates on human evolution intersect with U.S. missionary efforts funded, finally, by powerful and secretive organizations interested primarily in natural resources, and willing to bribe a geologist, deny a livelihood to an entire native population, and even risk nuclear war by protecting those interests.

In his essay on religion, Gaddis notices, with Carl Jung, that lapsed Catholics are likely to be absolute in their rejection of the faith, whereas Protestant rebellion permits variations. Through all his variations, Gaddis in his apostasy consistently leans to the side of his native Protestantism—which helps to explain the satirical quality of his work, the way he will seemingly reduce one idea or character to absurdity only to have that same idea or character appear positively, even heroically, later in the narrative, in light of other, equal and opposite absurdities. An aporia is also a blind spot. And Gaddis's genius lies partly in his ability to seek out culturally induced blind spots, not from some all-knowing position of authorial control, but rather by having one character (or the same character at a later time) reveal the blind spots of another, differently positioned character: Lester and McCandless in debates on religion, McCandless and Liz meeting and avoiding each other in love, Liz and Paul, Paul and Billy, Billy and McCandless. . . . The circulating, often mutually uncomprehending conversations may appear futile to the characters themselves. But we, the readers, not only see what they fail to see and fail to communicate; we are also able to see *how* they fail, and by making comparisons and exploring ambiguities in their words and their situations, we can begin to assemble a pattern, never conclusive, bespeaking larger forces and systems that condition their world.

The Work of Art and the Ecology
of Mass Media

From a "Protestant point of view," Gaddis finds Jung saying, when an individual's relation to God becomes "overpowered by mass organization," religion finds more "collective" expressions and feelings—and this, too, could describe the embattled personality behind Gaddis's affinity for systems and his willingness to submerge his own expression in the clichés of corporate speech. The power and profound sadness of the later work depends, implicitly, on the accumulated weight of the unpublished research— "the destructive element" in which Gaddis immersed himself for so long—which is sampled in this volume by selected notes from the player piano project arranged chronologically as an appendix. These are working papers, and throughout Gaddis refrains from commentary or elaboration. What we have instead is nothing but "the fact, man, the irrefragable fact" demanded by Jack London in his pursuit of a naturalist fiction appropriate to the age of Darwin, Nietzsche, and Mary Baker Eddy—three names whose sheer juxtaposition on the first legal-sized sheet of notes speaks volumes about the difficult integration of religion and science, fact and the fictions we will always need (Gaddis supposes) to "get us safely through the night." Though he may not have intended the effect, the absence of narrative in the notes produces a document reminiscent of the elusive work dreamed of by Walter Benjamin after he had neglected to complete the requirements for a professorship in Germany—a book that would consist of nothing but quotations from other books.

Gaddis had not read Benjamin on mechanization and the arts when I questioned him about this in 1990, but he came to acknowledge Benjamin's "pertinence" as yet another instance of convergence, not influence. Affinities between Gaddis and Benjamin have more to do with a certain attitude of mind than a shared philosophy, and a style that is not impersonal but rather speaks *through* modern materials, methods, and systems. By creating a pattern out of found material that is itself largely patternless, an author elaborates a consciousness in language that is always vehemently personal. Gaddis is as confessional as Anne Sexton. As much as anything he might say in the essays, their incomparable style sheds light on the literary mind in the making, and on how literature, an island of print in an electronic sea of information, communicates—and communicates *differently*. Gaddis's audience has been limited in part because readers trained on nineteenth-century realism miss in his work those signs and conventional symptoms by which characters may be recognized, too readily, as rounded and whole. Such conventional characters are agents within a bourgeois and industrial world that is now, in the United States, largely historical. In Gaddis's imagination, character, meaning, and agency come not from some essential, core self but from the languages and systems that circulate through many selves in a social collectivity—including the "self that could do more," a potential, creative agency that emerges only in the work, and in the act of recognizing answering patterns in the work of others.

The character Thomas Eigen, one of several Gaddis personae in *J R*, laments that his "very important book" was being read by only the "very small audience" for literary fiction. While this audience stubbornly persists, by now it may have dispersed to invisibility against the rise of commercial publishing. Yet there are other audiences, not strictly attuned in their tastes to the mass product and quite able to access the very good Gaddis Web site. He has always found readers among visual artists and art followers, some of whom are creating pieces that parallel Gaddis's own investigations, such as Tim Hawkinson's *Überorgan* at Mass Moca's *Unnatural Science* exhibition (2000–2001), an electronically driven pipe organ equipped with a yardwide, two-hundred-foot-long Mylar roll (using black paint instead of holes); or the projected charcoal drawings of William Kentridge, who develops his visual narratives in much the same way that Gaddis creates verbal transitions from one scene to the next—through telephone lines and office machinery and abstract forms generated from time and motion studies and informed by philosophies of modern science. Another example is Eve Andrée Laramée's spring 1999 installation at the MIT List Visual Arts Center, which displayed a binary-card-driven embroidery loom in an eighteenth-century period room, featuring wall portraits nearing photographic quality (at one thousand threads per inch) of Vaucanson's mechanical duck and flutist; Lord Byron's daughter Lady Ada Lovelace; her collaborator and the inventor of the first computer Charles Babbage; and Jacquard himself wearing a jacket covered with zeroes and ones. This is the very pantheon one finds portrayed in Gaddis's notes, throughout the essays and occasional writings, and in his final fiction, *Agapē Agape*, which appears, separately but concurrently, with this volume of critical writings.

Through such widespread, collaborating reconsiderations, these critical artists have been, like Gaddis, gradually constructing an alternative history of the arts in digital culture. The flourishing of the player piano, brought to a close by radio whose own star would be eclipsed, in turn, by video and TV, encapsulated for Gaddis the simultaneous waste and creativity within the culture of planned obsolescence. By closely following these intermedial struggles for representational dominance, Gaddis again makes failure and "the rush for second place" a principle means to success "precisely in the arts where one's best is never good enough." Even as his own widely referential, densely interlinked narratives anticipate hypertext, his particular sort of fiction, Gaddis knew, was both endangered and enlivened by the rise of new media and the business interests spawned by the media. He often said he felt a kinship with the bluebird—the onetime official bird of his home state, New York. This bird had been declared extinct but has since made a comeback. "For good reasons," Gaddis moralizes, the writer in the United States "has been and remains an endangered species. That is our edge."

In spite of affinities and mutual endangerments, however, Gaddis remained skeptical of art in his own time: indeed, he was not unsympathetic to the thwarted museumgoer who says "my five-year-old could do better." And so, while he credited his daughter, Sarah Gaddis, for the original watercolor on the jacket of *A Frolic of His Own*, he neglected to indicate that it was done when she was five years old. Not one of the book's reviewers seems to have noticed. Gaddis always knew how to play the confidence game with the experts. For a precursor and leading practitioner of postmodernism in American fiction he was remarkably traditional in his tastes and hesitant to participate in the markets and media he understood so well. He would eventually moderate his views on contemporary art, however, and he even came to consider the possibility of reading from his work. (Through most of his career he shared Christina's view in *Frolic*, that you read aloud to children.) He had always been on good terms with the artist Saul Steinberg, who lived nearby in Sag Harbor and whose own archive would be temporarily stored next to Gaddis's in a warehouse on Long Island City. (The archive was disposed, in the spring of 2002, with the collections at Washington University, St. Louis.) More surprisingly, Gaddis developed a close and lasting friendship with Julian Schnabel, the subject of his very last occasional piece. He admired Schnabel, evidently, for much the same reason that he was fond of the boy J R—for his entrepreneurial spirit, his commitment (talent or none), and his determination to seek every opportunity for his enterprise to "prevail." "Julian would be doing what he does no matter what," Gaddis would say: "He just gets so excited about things!"[5] As an expression of fellowship among artists, the piece on Schnabel makes for an appropriate conclusion to this volume. Especially touching is the prospect of Gaddis in his seventies introducing Schnabel—then in his forties—on the occasion of his receiving the Lifetime Achievement Award from the Guild Hall Academy of the Arts.

Gaddis, who was too frail to attend the ceremony, praised Schnabel's work for compelling us to "look, and look again." For it is here precisely, in the act of second-order observation, that the viewer or reader participates in the artist's creative vision. Schnabel in 1987 assembled Gaddis's portrait out of oil, broken plates, and bondo on wood. Is Schnabel in turn being portrayed in the tribute as yet another Gaddis persona? Another of his proliferating doubles? And whose eye is it—Schnabel's or Gaddis's—doing the twinkling in that last line of ambiguous prose? Look again.

N O T E S

1. Gaddis's collegiate parodies, many of them Elizabethan, were mostly written for the *Harvard Lampoon* and should one day be collected together as a separate volume. Future editors might also consider the "very early beginnings at fiction," which Gaddis intended "probably to be destroyed" but in fact kept together in a small carton.

2. From a letter to Gregory Comnes.

3. *Homo Ludens: A Study of the Play Element in Culture* (1938. English trans. 1949; rpt. Boston: Beacon Press, 1955), 111.

4. Gaddis's remarks at the St. Louis colloquium appear throughout the collection *The Writer and Religion*, edited by William H. Gass and Lorin Cuoco (Carbondale and Edwardsville: Southern Illinois University Press, 2000). He speaks of the Christian right on page 56.

5. Cited by Sarah Gaddis in "A Note of Gratitude" introducing a "William Gaddis Tribute" in *Conjunctions* 33 (1999): 150. Schnabel's 1987 portrait of Gaddis is reproduced on page 148.

THE RUSH FOR
SECOND PLACE

"STOP PLAYER. JOKE NO. 4"

GADDIS'S FIRST NATIONAL publication. An earlier version titled "You're a Dog Gone Daisy Girl—Presto" was submitted to *The New Yorker* when Gaddis worked there (1945–46) as a fact checker. The essay was rejected, but by that time he was already living in France and at work on *The Recognitions*. In 1950 he renewed his research and sent a more elaborate version of about thirty manuscript pages to *The Atlantic Monthly,* which, as he wrote in a letter to Helen Parker, "offered to take an excerpt from it, or possibly the whole." The excerpt appeared under the title " 'Stop Player. Joke No. 4' " in the July 1951 issue.

Drafts for other essays, along with a synopsis for television and half a dozen early attempts at fiction rejected by *The New Yorker* and *Harper's,* would remain boxed up for the next half century, indications of a literary life in letters Gaddis would not pursue. At some point he must have seen for himself—and avoided—the literary destiny given to a character in his early "Fable of a Fabricator," who moments after dying "felt that there must be someone to whom he should account for himself: eleven anthologies, sixteen introductions, and twelve years of interviews and reviews (he was still uncertain as to whether to call himself a critic)." In *The Recognitions,* rather than fabricate conventional fictions he explored the origins and impulse behind fabrication itself. He was not without his own aspirations as a

1

cultural critic, but he would not find a style for the player piano project until the early sixties, by which time he was too immersed in corporate and commercial writing to move ahead with the literary-historical project.

"STOP PLAYER. JOKE NO. 4"

Selling player pianos to Americans in 1912 was not a difficult task. There was a place for everyone in this brave new world, where the player offered an answer to some of America's most persistent wants: the opportunity to participate in something which asked little understanding; the pleasure of creating without work, practice, or the taking of time; and the manifestation of talent where there was none.

Age was no hindrance to success. A child in Seattle who had spent his full five years among players was an expert demonstrator.

A number of magazines devoted to the player—many of them put out by the manufacturers themselves—were stolidly enough written to convince any player owner that his was the most important instrument in the history of music and that he was its master. The *Presto Buyers' Guide* kept him up on new developments and new rolls, and the *Player* magazine threatened to educate him to his machine.

One of its regular columns was "Music Roll Thematics," reproducing the patterns of various groups of holes from familiar classic rolls, and tossing in ten good reasons why they were important, as well as a story of the composition. The idea was to read the groups of perforations while playing the roll, as the professional musician reads notes; and music presented in these new working clothes became something which was perhaps tangible after all.

Player programs were suggested for less imaginative owners, who soon learned not to compromise themselves artistically in an evening's entertainment by mixing such popular works as Swift's *Rag Medley No. 8* and Gottschalk's *The Dying Poet* with light opera classics from Van Alsteyne's *Girlies* or Karl Hoschna's *Madame Sherry.*

The industry, probably largely out of respect, built 10,000 grands in 1914, but out of the 325,000 total, 80,000 were player pianos. Piano repairmen, who had started their vocation with nothing to fear from the regularities of the pianoforte, were encouraged with books, folders, and diagrams explaining the wonders of pneumatics. That year the Danquard Player Action School opened in New York, giving exhaustive courses in player mechanics, and there were even a few correspondence schools peddling the new profession.

The roll industry had been a necessary accomplice throughout, but it had an attraction all its own. The notion of transforming any piece of music, from a ditty to a concerto, into an anonymous series of holes on a blank paper roll was as exciting for some as cuneiform investigation. The roll industry grew as fast as the player world would permit, though some player companies kept the business in the family and cut their own rolls. Such artists as Robert Wornum and Emanuel Moór were to be found cutting "records" for Aeolian, Ampico, and Welte-Mignon. The smallest Leabarjan perforator cost $35, and with it one could make one's own paper music. One man patented an oilcloth roll, and another, equally imaginative, settled down with a punch and a roll of wallpaper.

Most light-minded people turned to the Arto-roll or the Vocalstyle. The Arto-roll was so named because the space usually left blank at the end where the roll tapered to the ring was filled with art work and comment. After a spirited performance of the sextet from *Lucia,* the fugitive slots rolled out of sight as usual before the spectator's eyes, and he and anyone else who wanted to crowd around were presented with a chromo of lolling maidens and a snappy discourse on the tribulations of the heroine.

James Whitcomb Riley bought a player in 1905, and as poetic consequence the Vocalstyle Company printed up some of his work to be sold and recited with rolls of their own music in accompaniment. They also produced one-roll minstrel shows, on which the procession of slots was interrupted by the words "Stop Player. Joke No. 4." At this point, the jokebook which came with the roll was opened to Joke No. 4. A proper parlor version of Mr. Interlocator then opened some such extended discussion as this:—

"You say you got a dog that doan' eat meat?"

"Yuphm," a partner answered.

"Why doan' your dog eat no meat?"

"Cuz I doan' give him no meat"—and the player piano burst out again over shrieks of parlor laughter. Words to the songs were printed on the roll, and for wordless sequences such as a soft-shoe dance, encouraging exclamations were freely supplied:—

"Throw sand on the floor and give him room!"

Or, "Conserve shoe leather! Conserve!"

The Age of Gold lasted through 1916, when popular parlor players were rendering *Ragtime Oriole, Way Down in Borneo-*

o-o-o, and *You're a Dog Gone Daisy Girl*. Talents were being made and recognized. The makers of a roll called *Posies* testified, in reference to Dorian Welch, the composer, "There is a special talent in writing for the player piano, and but few writers possess it." In addition to Mr. Welch, Paul Hindemith and Erik Satie directed some of their "special talents" to player composing, and Satie even cut a few rolls.

The player actually became the biggest factor in the entire music industry, and Aeolian's prices on its Orchestrelle ranged from $400 to $3,500.

More than 200,000 player pianos were built in 1916. They amounted to 65 percent of the total piano production, enough to satisfy the most ardent fanatic and to warn anyone familiar with business graph curves of the impending decline and fall.

AGAPĒ AGAPE: THE SECRET
HISTORY OF THE PLAYER PIANO

EVIDENTLY THE INTRODUCTION to the projected historical work. Much of this essay appears, in fragments, as Jack Gibbs's failed project in *J R*. Although Gaddis had kept perhaps one hundred pages from earlier drafts and he anticipated (at this stage) a finished work approaching fifty thousand words, these few introductory pages are all that Gaddis was ready to show the world. Brief though it is, the essay is complete and it stands as the closest indication of what he had in mind for the player piano project. (A project summary given to his agent in the early sixties appears as an Appendix, along with notes transcribed from Gaddis's working papers.)

In one of the drafts, Gaddis had cited the Broadway stage writer William Saroyan on the "razzle-dazzle" quality of the best piano rolls. That was their "greatness," said Saroyan: "The 'serious' rolls stink of course." A certain seriousness and a bizarre snobbery in Gaddis's own early discursive style perhaps needed to be shed before he could make headway on any project dealing with technology and the "false democratization of the arts." Even the passages Gibbs reads aloud from this draft still sound "difficult" to every character in *J R* who is made to hear them. Gibbs realizes that the work was not "written to be read aloud," and he knows too that most people would "rather be at the movies" than sit alone reading a social history of the player piano, or a novel for that matter.

The wavering tone of this short essay, a mixture of erudition and tavern wit appropriate to the subject, is in part a response to these medial pressures. But by the time Gaddis solved the stylistic problem of writing about technology, he had left behind the player piano to work on another project, a "novel about business" conceived in 1957 that would become *J R* (letter to John D. Seelye, February 2, 1963). Gaddis avoided tonal problems that plague the early nonfiction by writing the novel almost entirely in dialogue, recycling as art the clichés, false starts, stutters, sound bites, and other waste products of the programmatic culture itself. Once he'd decided to go this route, he had no hesitation in breaking up the short essay he had labored over, and presenting it, through Gibbs, in a form more fragmentary than the original, which appears here for the first time.

AGAPĒ AGAPE

The Secret History of the Player Piano

PLEASE DO NOT SHOOT THE
PIANIST
HE IS DOING HIS BEST

Posted in a Leadville saloon, this appeal caught the passing eye of Art in its ripe procession of one through the new frontier of the eighties, where the frail human element still abounded even in the arts themselves. "The mortality among pianists in that place is marvellous," Oscar Wilde observed: was it that *doing his best* which rankled? redolent of chance and the very immanence of human failure that that century of progress was consecrated to wiping out once for all; for if, as another mother-country throwback had it, all art does constantly aspire toward the condition of music, there in a Colorado mining-town saloon all art's essential predicament threatened to be laid bare with the clap of a pistol shot just as deliverance was at hand, born of the beast with two backs called Arts and Sciences whose rambunctious coupling came crashing the jealous enclosures of class, taste, and talent, to open the arts to Americans for democratic action and leave history to bunk.

"A remarkable characteristic of the Americans is the manner in which they have applied science to modern life," Wilde marveled, struck by "the noisiest country that ever existed. One is waked up in the morning, not by the singing of the nightingale, but by the steam whistle. . . . All Art depends upon exquisite and delicate sensibility, and such constant turmoil must ultimately be destructive of the musical faculty." And thus, though "the flute is not an instrument which is expressive of moral character; it is too exciting," it was not Aristotle's rebuke that had checked young Frank Woolworth's rash ambitions on the instrument: he was becomingly tone-deaf, and by 1879 had already crowned a decade of insolvency with the failure of his 5 cent store in Utica, New York, his musical faculty engulfed in an atmosphere where the wages of leisure were being advertised by McGuffey's fourth *Eclectic Reader* in terms of George Jones, last glimpsed as "a poor wanderer, without money and without friends. Such are the wages of idleness. I hope every reader will, from this history, take warning, and 'stamp improvement on the wings of time.' "

Pursued by the crippled ghost of exquisite and delicate sensibility, Frank Woolworth fled to new enterprise in Lancaster Pa. to inflict ambition where his best would be good enough, securing success with a line of 10¢ items and stamping his nickel-and-dime improvement on the democracy even then being flushed on wings of song from elsewhere in Aristotle's lecture notes where it had, all this time, been pinioned as a forlorn delusion rising "out of the notion that those who are equal in any respect are equal in all."

Roused by the steam whistle, democracy's claims devoured technology's promise, banishing failure to inherent vice where in painting it remains today, and America sprang full in the face of that dead philosopher's reproach "to be always seeking after the useful does not become free and exalted souls." By the nineties the arts had already begun their retirement at Hull House, where they were introduced as therapy, while in the streets the discovery of Spencer's "immutable law" drove Jack London howling "Give me the fact, man! The irrefragable fact!"

Pragmatically, as pragmatism passed, William James grabbed it, as literature unfolded to catalogue the phenomena that oppressed Maggie, the Girl of the Streets, which John Dewey was groping at for educational purposes, "the close and intimate acquaintance got with nature at first hand, with real things and materials, with the actual processes of their manipulation, and the knowledge of their social necessities and uses." Fresh from such manipulations in the cellar of James' Cambridge house, E. L. Thorndike emerged with his book *Animal Intelligence*, laying the foundations for testing in our modern public schools in terms of intelligent behavior in chickens, terms that could be measured and compared as time and motion were being straitjacketed in a Bethlehem steel plant by F. W. Taylor, terms that could be sorted, weighed, and evaluated as readily as the items on Frank Woolworth's expanding counters, tangibility which could be classified and organized, as Mary Baker Eddy was efficiently demonstrating even while insisting it did not exist, organization whose smooth functioning the shoe machinery trust made clear was as much a part of the shoe machinery industry as the reciprocal gears of the shoe machinery itself.

Disappointed with Niagara, "—most people must be disappointed with Niagara," consoled on that jaunt only by the fact that such an artist as Madame Bernhardt had allowed herself to be photographed in just such an ungainly yellow mackintosh as he was forced to wear, Oscar Wilde still knew "no country in the world where machinery is so lovely as in America. I have always wished to believe that the line of strength and the line of beauty are one. That wish was realised when I contemplated American machinery. It was not until I had seen the water-works at Chicago that I realised the wonders of machinery; the rise and fall of the steel rods, the symmetrical motion of great wheels is the most beautifully rhythmic thing I have ever seen."

Spread broadcast, this aesthetic experience of Wilde's was leveling men's claims to being absolutely equal since they were absolutely free, the symmetrical motion of those great wheels homogenizing their differences till by the time Horatio Alger died the hand at the machine had a distinctly childish cast, and Ragged Dicks were everywhere, one in seven children between ten and fifteen out working for wages, a body thirty times the size of the U.S. Army for whom refinements on Cartwright's loom and advances in canning machinery and the glass industry swelled the coercion of equal opportunity to the turgid proportions Alger himself left behind in 119 works, a generation indoctrinated "in the comforting assurance that virtue is always rewarded by wealth and honour," and a century labeled "one of the most fascinating chapters in the story of man's upward progress" by one of the survivors, Reverend Newell Dwight Hillis. "For the first time government, invention, art, industry, and religion have served all the people rather than the patrician classes.

"The millions join in the upward march."

And while those millions saw where they were marching much as Mark Twain saw them "through a glass eye, darkly," the one-eyed man could now peer into Aristotle's kingdom where, "if every instrument could accomplish its own work, obeying or anticipating the will of others, like the statues of Daedalus, or the tripods of Hephaestus, which, says the poet, 'of their own accord entered the assembly of the gods'; if, in like manner, the shuttle would weave and the plectrum touch the lyre without a hand to guide them, chief workmen would not want servants, nor masters slaves." For though the tale how for art's sake Wilde had faced Leadville's bullies to a standstill continued to amuse long after he'd withdrawn to join the compost smouldering in Europe with Pater's recipe for "success in life," here, now mother of necessity, invention was eliminating the very possibility of failure as a condition for success precisely in the arts where one's best is never good enough and who, so armed, could resist the temptation to shoot the pianist if the song would play on without losing a note?

"The only rational method of art criticism I have ever come across," said Wilde, now elsewhere and dead, a "mildewed chump," and Stephen Crane who'd called him that dead too, as up

the marble staircase of Frank Woolworth's new Fifth Avenue mansion the twentieth century stalked and broke over the new Lao-
coön to the life, sitting there numbed in a forest of player piano
rolls while lights of various hues lofted, on tones steeped from a
vast player pipe organ without a hand to guide them, that hardy
ghost of "exquisite and delicate sensibility" up, up to heights at
which a bat must seem an angel to a mouse.

The music of the world is free to all.
For those whom classic pieces interest, Scarlatti, Bach, Haydn,
and old Handel have written oratorios and fugues. Unhappy
Schubert speaks to them in the sweet tones of Rosamunde.
Beethoven, master of masters, thrills alike the listeners and
the performer with his Appassionata or beautiful Fifth
Symphony.
  Chopin bemoans the fate of Poland in his Nocturnes or
breathes the fiery valor of his countrymen in Polonaise.
Mendelssohn, Rubinstein, Moszkowski, Liszt, all help to weave
tone-pictures for ear and mind alike to revel in. For other tastes,
where settings of the stage have served to spur the fancies of
their favorites, great Wagner comes and, lifting them aloft above
the clouds, transports them to the mighty Halls of old Walhalla,
in Ride of Walküres, or takes them to the cool, green depths of
classic Rhine in Nibelungen Ring . . .
  The Pianola is the universal means of playing the piano.
Universal, because there is no one in all the world, having the
use of hands and feet, who could not learn to use it with but
little effort . . .
  The striking of the notes of the selection, in proper time and
place, is no concern of the player. This is correctly done by perforated rolls of paper . . .

And there, in 1902, the tangible essence of the programmed republic 2,289 years and all the civilized West in the making, lay waiting execution in the century ahead. Analysis, measurement, prediction and control, the elimination of failure through programmed organization, the player emerged as a distillation of the goals that had surrounded its gestation in an orgy of fragmented talents seeking after the useful, Rockefeller organizing this world as Darwin the last one and Mrs. Eddy the next, Pullman organizing people and Spies labor, Eastman and McCormick patents and parts, Woolworth cash and Morgan credit, Frick power with his own property and Insull with other people's, Gibbs physics, Comstock vice, and Hollerith the census, while Spencer programmed ethics and Freud the psyche, Taylor work, Dewey facts, James things, Mendel, Correns, Tschermak and De Vries and De Vries, Tschermak and Correns heredity, a frenzied search for just those patterns in communication and control that were even then not only transporting Frank Woolworth's damaged musical faculty "hatless, dishevelled and gay" in Ride of Walküres to the mighty Halls of old Walhalla, but carrying all the people rather than the patrician classes toward the utopian equilibrium of John Stuart Mills's stationary state, where the stream of human industry will "finally spread itself out into an apparently stagnant sea."

TREATMENT FOR A MOTION PICTURE ON "SOFTWARE"

PREPARED FOR THE IBM World Trade Corporation, this treatment is an example of the kind of film Gaddis scripted for various corporations—Eastman Kodak and Pfizer Pharmaceuticals as well as IBM—and for the United States Army during the period 1961–70. Not all of his pieces found acceptance. There exists in the archives a letter of evaluation from a Mr. A. E. Jeffcoat, whose name would not have been out of place in a Gaddis novel: "Better organization," Jeffcoat notes on an early draft of an IBM educational brochure, "simpler style (shorter words, sentences, paragraphs) seem in order. The whole of the text is perhaps too much an impenetrable mass." Gaddis himself, reflecting on a commission from the Ford Foundation for a film on the use of closed-circuit television in classrooms, found himself "between two stools, huzzahs for the tonic effect [the technology] is having in (public school) teaching interspersed with caveats on technology devouring its own children, all this complicated by constant notes and thoughts and reading on the side on *my* book started many years ago largely on this same area, technology/democracy/the artist" (letter to John D. Seelye, February 2, 1963).

The Ford Foundation project eventually fell through after pointless travel, rejected drafts, and the eventual kill fee. (His experience would be given to the characters aptly named Ford and Gall in *J R*). Most of his corporate work was well received, however, and often he was able to ventriloquize his own views and opinions through the executives who delivered his commissioned speeches. In professional life, as in fiction, he was inclined to speak through mouthpieces, even as he would give to the characters in his books—a coldhearted business mogul, a snot-nosed preadolescent—words he might believe in but would never have said himself. At the same time, he was able frequently to work in literary allusions—to Thoreau on technology as "an improved means to an unimproved end," to Max Weber on society's decline from Status to Contract with the rise of capital, and, in the closing line of the film script printed below, to Gertrude Stein on the circularity of programmed culture, which is only capable of answering questions that it has already formulated.

Although most of the corporate writings were impersonal and technical, Gaddis could not entirely repress a narrative impulse. A film sequence meant to illustrate a concept in information science—the way an entire city impinges on a man's decision to cross a street—becomes in Gaddis's hands a mini-narrative culminating in the black humor of a crash. Soon thereafter, we're given footage of a collapsing bridge. The environment of noise, accident, uncertainty, and failure so characteristic of Gaddis may have been more than his sponsors bargained for. This particular script was never produced.

While Gaddis made enough money at commercial writing to support his family throughout the sixties, the work—and, not least, the temptations of expense account living—kept him from finishing both the player piano project and the "novel on business" he had "begun and dropped" in 1957. Evidently, by this

time Gaddis was also well into the civil war project that would find
its way into *A Frolic of His Own*: "a novel begun, rebuilt into an im-
possibly long play (very rear guard, Socrates in the U.S. Civil War),
shelved 1960." And still, he had hopes of finding a publisher for
his "current obsession with expanding prospects of programmed
society & automation in the arts which may bring in advance, a
commitment, even an escape from the tomb of the 9-to-5"(letter
to John Seelye, May 21, 1962 [originally May 18]).

He never was able to interest a publisher in the nonfiction
project; by the end of the sixties, though, he secured an advance
(extended and then bought out and renewed by a second publisher) and a National Endowment for the Arts (NEA) grant allowing him to work full time on the novel *J R*. Even then, however,
Gaddis would be so in need of money that he would ghostwrite
articles for a dentist in exchange for root canals. His son recalls
one day happening to find his checkbook, and noting the balance, meticulously calculated, of twelve cents. This was at the
time when Gaddis had just won the 1976 National Book Award.

TREATMENT FOR A MOTION
PICTURE ON "SOFTWARE"

Prepared for IBM World Trade Corp.
Writer: William Gaddis

The motion picture opens with a scene of a man happily playing
the piano—or so it appears, though we cannot see his hands on the

keys. When this scene is established, the off-screen Narrator states that this is a film about problem solving, and observes that almost any problem can be solved that can be stated adequately.

This man, he continues, has a problem. His problem is that he enjoys the piano but is unable to play it. At this, we cut to a shot of the man at the piano from behind, revealing the fact that he is simply going through the motions with his hands, and the instrument, a player piano, is being "played" by a punched paper piano roll.

This sequence opens the introductory portion of the film which, by analogy, establishes the relationship between "software" and "hardware," in information systems designed to solve problems. The uselessness of the hardware without the software becomes abruptly apparent as the piano roll flaps loudly, the keys stop moving, and the music ends.

There is no mystery in such systems, only complexity, the Narrator continues, as the camera shows in close-up the player's internal workings, a complex tangle of tubes and bellows. And in narration, which parallels but does not refer directly to the instrument on the screen, the Narrator describes the way in which remarkable results may be produced by various problem-solving apparatus from the most essentially simple data and instructions.

The mere "on" or "off," "yes" or "not-yes" response made possible by, for example, holes punched in paper or cards, allowing air to pass through and activate a bellows, or electricity to close a contact, may be made to act as an instruction to a machine to perform some single simple function, such as striking a string with a hammer. On split screen, we are shown the holes in the piano roll passing over the tracker bar, and the hammers striking the piano strings, as the piano's music continues as background to the narration.

Such simple functions, the Narrator continues, as striking a string with a hammer to produce a musical note, have little meaning unless resolved into patterns with other notes which resolve the problem, in this case, to produce music. Other problems involve other solutions and other sorts of patterns, those woven into cloth for example. And now, as the Narrator describes this long and painstaking process when done by hand, the details of tapestry weaving as pictured in Diderot's famous eighteenth-century encyclopedia appear on the screen.

The problem of conducting this operation more rapidly and economically can also be solved if the process can be broken down into single steps which may be converted into simple, single instructions for a machine, exactly, in fact, as it was resolved by Jacquard's punch-card loom back at the beginning of the nineteenth century. And here the scene on the screen dissolves to bad prints of Jacquard's loom of 1804.

The essence of problem solving, the Narrator continues, is the ability to envision the elements that will compose the solution. When these elements are arranged, or "programmed," in single logical steps leading toward the solution, these steps may then be converted into sequential instructions for the machine to follow. And as the camera comes in to a close-up of the linked punch cards on the Jacquard loom, the Narrator points out that this, in turn, is the essence of what we call "software" in our modern computer information systems. It is the medium used for communicating the elements of the problem and of its solution to the problem-solving machine.

Thus, the Narrator goes on, almost any problem can be solved that can be adequately stated. And here a point is made which is stressed throughout the film: that even modern complex language and logic systems cannot solve anything that human beings cannot program.

How this is done, of course, is determined by the workings and capabilities of the machine, or hardware, the computer in modern information systems. Transition from software to hardware is accomplished on the screen by moving from piano roll and punched card (to punched paper tape) as the means used for Input, introducing the sequence on the computer.

With the help of animation, the computer's capabilities and basic operations are presented briefly and succinctly, its capabilities being to add, subtract, multiply, divide, and compare; its basic operations Input, Storage, Processing, and Output.

The point is made in the narration that even in complex modern language and logic machines, the *techniques* of logic themselves contain no meaning. The meaning remains outside the system. The problem-solving capability of the computer is keyed to the fact that if the problem can be logically defined, it can be expressed in terms of electric circuitry. Here, the "on" or "off," "yes" or "not-yes" material from the introductory scenes of the film are used to introduce the binary number system employed in computer operation. The step-by-step nature of this operation is shown on the screen in the form of light paths moving through the branches of a "logic tree"* in a series of "on" or "off" alternatives of electrical circuits. Having made the point of the step-by-step nature of software programming and computer operation, the "logic tree" of moving light paths becomes an extremely effective method of demonstrating computer speeds on the screen.

---

*Such a logic tree demonstration is available at the IBM Washington Presentation Center.

Illustrated by live action, the computer's memory and logic system, and the functions of information storage and retrieval, are presented in terms stressing their importance in the information system. The point is emphasized on the screen and in the narration, however, that the computer itself is no more than a complicated network as useless as a random stack of wire and transistor circuits until its behavior is organized by a systematic coded memory, to make it a "general purpose machine," and that it is the software program that transforms this into a "highly specialized immensely fast calculating tool, custom built to do a particular job economically."

The particular job, of course, depends upon the particular problem, the Narrator continues over shots on the screen of Output in the form of screen and rapid printing, concluding the computer sequence. Problem solving and decision making are processes familiar to all of us. They occur in our lives every minute of the day.

Crossing the street, for example, the Narrator goes on, as we see on the screen the man from the film's opening player piano sequence, now poised on the curb of an empty two-lane street. You simply look both ways and, if nothing is coming, you cross. But . . . the Narrator continues, as we cut to the same figure poised on the curb of a crowded city street, and the Narrator enumerates possible factors involved in the solution to this pedestrian's problem. The distance across the street and his estimated time in crossing it, for example, figured against the length of the light and speed of the traffic. Then, as the Narrator adds possible variables, these appear on the screen: a cyclist, a delivery cart, an ambulance, a right-turning cab; and, on the pedestrian's part, contingencies which pop up on the screen as they are named: he may have luggage; the luggage may include a pair of skis; he may have had a skiing accident, and crutches.

The one way he cannot attempt to solve his problem, the Narrator notes, is by trial and error. As he says this, the encumbered pedestrian steps from the curb, cars come head-on into the camera, there is the blare of horns and squeal of brakes, and silence.

This, on the other hand, is precisely what the computer language and logic system can do. As we have noted, the Narrator continues, almost any problem can be solved that can be adequately stated. Preparing this detailed step-by-step statement of data and instructions, and including in it every variation of every possible contingency, is what we have called programming, and the programmed software can be manipulated in the computer like a model of the real situation until, by trial and error, the problem is resolved. And over a series of still shots or freeze-frames from the preceeding pedestrian's dilemma, the Narrator goes on to note that before programming, fundamental questions must be posed and answered: Is the job necessary? Is it suited to the computer? Is it worth being done by computer in terms of time saved? Is it adaptable to existing programs? Is it unique?

And as an example of a problem situation less complex and desperate than that of the pedestrian, we turn to the dinner-party planning sequence taken from the IBM film *View from the People Wall*, in which a woman is shown planning the seating of her guests by trial and error. The Narrator points out the parallel in her approach to preparing computer software: stating the problem; collecting the information; abstracting the information; building the model; and manipulating the model.

Where the pattern of behavior can be defined, he goes on, every problem can be translated into a statistical or mathematical model, to act out all the parts of the problem in detail and predict the results of a particular series of decisions. Since, as we have seen, the machine works one step at a time, on the basis of "on" or "off," "yes" or "not-yes" circuitry, it is the programmer's work to arrange the problem in logical steps, stated in unambiguous language translatable into the 1's and 0's of the binary system.

Actual software preparation is begun by preparing a flow chart, the Narrator continues, as we see a flow chart being prepared on the screen. The problem being approached here is the design for a bridge, and the Narrator describes the way in which individual programmers are assigned parts of the master plan to transform into hundreds of logical steps, the testing of these separate programs, and then of all the programs together.

As this description of software preparation proceeds, we see on the screen stress-strain patterns associated with simulation in bridge design as they appear on a computer monitor screen. As the Narrator discusses computer manipulation of mathematical models, an inset appears on the motion picture screen to one side of the monitor. In this motion picture inset, we see a real bridge swaying under wind and stress. This inset grows larger as the Narrator continues. As he makes the point that the purpose of computer manipulation of mathematical models is to avoid the possible unhappy consequences of trial and error in reality, the inset fills the screen and the bridge is shown collapsing.*

Obviously, the Narrator now notes, since each bit of data and instruction must be encoded for the computer's step-by-step operation, a single program represents a very great deal of work. One Applications Program may contain 25,000 instructions. But pre-

---

*Film footage of a major bridge collapse is available for this sequence.

cisely what makes the preparation of such software possible is the fact that any large system becomes manageable when it is broken down into a number of single, simple decisions.

During this discussion by the Narrator, we see on the screen another sequence taken from the IBM film *View from the People Wall*, in which railroad car handling is shown as a large intricate system broken up into innumerable separate decisions.

As complex as such software preparation is, however, the Narrator goes on, once these programs are completed they may be used repeatedly for the same applications, and modified for problems containing similar elements. Thus he points out the number and variety of available software packages, the proliferation of software libraries, and the entire new industry of software producers that has emerged. At the same time, he notes the growing demands on computer software, and cites figures projecting the shortage of qualified programmers into the future.

From here, the film proceeds to review recent computer and software developments which have made the hardware-software relationship more complex and intimate, and tremendously augmented the capacities of these information systems. Whereas formerly, programs were fed into computers one by one, like piano rolls, increased speeds of computers have demanded constantly more sophisticated programming in order to cut down expensive "idle time." Much of modern computer and software advances center about systems which make it possible for the computer to program itself.

The concept of Operating Systems is presented on the screen as a series of transparent Lucite boxes of increasing dimensions, each of which is inscribed with appropriate mathematical formulae and fits over the next, as one system contains another of smaller complexity and capability.* The Narrator points out that such systems enable the computer user to concentrate more on his own problems and proportionately less on those brought about by the limitations of the machine. These increased systems capabilities have made possible the dramatic and complex development of concurrent access, in which one hundred or more users with different requirements may employ the same system.

In these systems, processing programs consisting of language translators and the user's own program, are executed under the supervision of a central program. Programs in the Operating System keep track of the rest of the system, and decide which of the applications in the system to act on first, processing one application while waiting for new input in others and scheduling the output at any of the various terminals connected to the system. A number of computers may also share one common storage device, two or more central processing units sharing a core containing one million bits of information.

This sequence on the computer's expanded capabilities is illustrated with suitable applications, including computer use at airports to keep as many as three hundred airplanes under control at one time, and the computer network which tabulated the results of the Winter Olympics at Grenoble.

The concluding sequence of the film re-emphasizes the intimate relationship between hardware and software in modern information systems and those ahead. In the fifties, instructions given the computer were written in langage adapted to the machine. In the sixties, capabilities built into the software made it

---

*The set of Lucite boxes designed to illustrate this concept is available at the IBM Presentation Center in Washington, D.C.

possible for computer users to develop languages more suited to the problems to be solved. Developments in both hardware and software point to a future near at hand in which computer processors will write the programs, from language suited to the user.

These growing demands upon the growing capabilities of these complex language and logic systems have also reduced Operator intervention, at the same time heightening the Operator's responsibility and importance, and the demands on his knowledge and training, for the proper functioning of the system.

The film concludes with a montage made up of shots from earlier scenes depicting problems and problem solving, as the Narrator points out that, however complex it becomes, the most advanced information system will still have human programming as the source of its problem-solving function.

Now on the screen we see examples of computer Output: screen, rapid printing, typewriter, and, finally, voice. In close-up, the hand of the Operator places a template over the keys on a telephone terminal, and punches the appropriate keys as the Narrator repeats that almost any problem that can be stated adequately can be solved, and that the essence of problem solving lies in the ability to envision the elements that will compose the solution, and even that must be organized by programming. Here, for example, is the unorganized vocabulary of the computer. And as the camera holds on the audio response unit, we hear the woman's voice recital of the vocabulary stored in the computer.

As this voice fades down and under, that of the Narrator locates the essence of software, and the heart of all language and logic systems, in the dying words of Gertrude Stein, when she asked "What is the answer?," and her friend professed ignorance. "In that case," she said, "what is the question?"

COVER ILLUSTRATIONS FROM THE
CORPORATE WRITINGS
(A SELECTION)

A SELECTION OUT OF TWO BOXES of corporate writings including (as Gaddis noted): "Outlines, notes, finished versions of film scripts written for the U.S Army (early 60s); same for executive speeches written for IBM, Eastman Kodak (late 60s)." The photograph illustrating the education pamphlet—a boy at a table with a Bible, a key, a pencil, and a voting ballot—is offered here as one possible model for the character J R. Equally resonant are Gaddis's fourth-grade compositions ("There is Lots of coal in Pennsylvania. There are lots of trains in Pennsylvania . . .") and his letters from boarding school to his mother, mostly itemizing needs and his accomplishments for the day.

The
GROWTH
of
AMERICAN
INDUSTRY

INDUSTRY AND THE AMERICAN ECONOMY • *Number One*

Americans have given their lives for the Constitutionally-protected rights represented by these physical symbols: freedom of religion; protection from unreasonable search and seizure; freedom of speech; representative government.

This is the first booklet in the series *Industry and the American Economy*. It has been written to show the development and place of industry in our way of life.

First Printing September 1959

EDUCATION DEPARTMENT
NATIONAL ASSOCIATION OF MANUFACTURERS
2 East 48th Street, New York 17, N. Y.

THE GROWTH OF AMERICAN INDUSTRY

PROLOGUE AND PROMISE

Suppose you *did* meet a man from Mars. One who accepted nothing at face value and wanted everything described and explained. Suppose also that he asked you what makes the United States so attractive that millions of people have migrated here voluntarily and tens of thousands more want to come each year. What would you say?

That it is a large country? He could point to China, the Soviet Union, Canada, Brazil — all physically larger.

That we have a large population? He would know that China, India and Soviet Russia each have more people.

That we have variety in our climate and in our natural resources? So do other countries with large areas.

That we have been responsible for many inventions and scientific discoveries? What about Bessemer, Watt, Nobel, Benz, Rutherford — and hundreds more from other countries who contributed to the industrial and scientific "revolutions" of the last two centuries?

That we have had representative government for a long time? London is the seat of the Mother of Parliaments.

That we have a high material standard of living? This is a result, not an explanation.

No. If you and your visitor from Mars went through a very long list of such possibilities you would probably end up with a very different answer. What makes this country unusual is the extent to which our people have had freedom and opportunity, under law, to do what they can—and will—with their lives. Your visitor would have to understand that a history and tradition of freedom and opportunity set the pattern for living today and determine what we want for tomorrow.

You would recommend that the man from Mars read the Declaration of Independence and the Constitution to become familiar with the principles and framework of the system under which we live. Freedom and opportunity are not physical things, although you could show him their effects and, even, physical symbols of their importance. But it is only in our everyday lives that one can see the real significance of freedom and opportunity.

The Declaration of Independence and the Constitution are both political documents. The Constitution describes a form of government and the limitations on the powers of that government. But the United States has not developed as it has merely because we are a people free *from* undue governmental interference and restriction. Opportunity *to* is the second essential. We have had the opportunity to make the most of the land, the resources, the climate, the qualities of people.

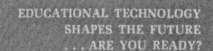

EDUCATIONAL TECHNOLOGY
SHAPES THE FUTURE
. . . ARE YOU READY?

An address by Mr. Gerald B. Zornow,
Vice President, Eastman Kodak Company,
to the National Catholic Educational Association

October 22, 1968

ANSWERS
TO CANCER

BY WILLIAM GADDIS

IN THE ZONE

AN ACCOUNT OF HIS DAYS in Central America "written thirty years later when American control of the Canal Zone was in dispute," this brief memoir remains Gaddis's "only excursion into autobiography" (Steven Moore). It appeared in *The New York Times* (on March 13, 1978) and was reprinted in Moore's *Reader's Guide to* The Recognitions.

IN THE ZONE

The point that winter thirty years ago was plainly just to get out of New York; and since an older brother of an affable boy I'd known in college owned Panama's leading bilingual newspaper, it seemed only logic to launch my international news career there with Tony's note recommending me, and the notes another classmate whose father had been a President of Panama—it was that kind of a college—wrote to friends, and to be welcomed by three or four of them in white dinner jackets fresh from a party the night I stepped off the plane.

They settled me into a large balconied room in the Hotel Central; a day or so later Roberto had me to lunch and sent me off to his managing editor who'd launched his own career in Australia and long since seen it all—and right there—with his brief review of my year's drudgery on a New York magazine and my eager struggle with Spanish—mine was ended from that day to this.

With it of course went any hope of immediate income; and with that, the room overlooking the Plaza de la Catedral for one in a barracks bungalow in Pedro Miguel, and the broken streets of Panama City for the clean lawns of the Canal Zone, where I got taken on as a machinist's assistant for the spring overhaul of the Miraflores locks.

Walking past Pedro Miguel's identical frame houses you could follow Sunday evening's radio—Jack Benny's remonstrance from one, Rochester's wail from the next—without missing a laugh.

The library was not only inexplicably well stocked, there was never the problem of any book of real depth or merit being out on loan. What writing and reading went on in our compound seemed mainly to be pencil-written responses to letters addressed there in pencil from home with a Southern postmark, relieved now and then by a penciled plea from some nearby country opening, "Why don't you say me?," and closing, "I will be jealous with all the womans of the world," even as the stuff for similar rebukes was being renewed on regular night jaunts across the line. That was the reason you went into Panama.

At that end, my new bondage in the Zone was seen as a lark. Nights off, my first cordial reception grew into dinner-and-dance at the Union Club; days off, trips in convertibles to beaches up the coast. Failing that, there was the long solitary lunch on a veranda of the old Hotel Tivoli just inside the Zone where of course *they* never came, awash in heavy napkins and silver and aging waiters cowed by uniforms and Zonians who sunburned heavily but never seemed to tan, the noon rain crashing down through the palms almost in reach and the specter of the 2 A.M. can of sardines, can of beans warmed on the base of a steam crane, no further than the change of clothes.

After a week or so sorting nuts and bolts by size, when it came clear that my grasp of machinery was even more vague than my Spanish I was put on at night running a small crane dangling an open elevator down the bite of the lock's gate to the canal floor eighty feet below. Since I couldn't see my passengers, two or three real machinists restoring the plates that sealed the gates watertight when they closed, my helper perched out where he could and relayed their hand signals to me in the dark, and I had finally to ask him to put on a white work glove so I could tell his up signal from down.

His name was Murrell. He was on the silver payroll at $18 a week and I made $65 on the gold payroll: convenient euphemisms held over from the building of the canal when, I had it explained, white workers were paid in gold, local labor in silver. These survived now on our pay slips, simply marked Gold and Silver, like the separate work elevators down the lock walls, but the silver payroll's separate drinking fountains were a forthright brown.

We wore that decade's shallow aluminum version of hard hats blazoned, as in every job and war since, with signs or sobriquets. Mine bore two discreet unlinked half-moons, Murrell's introduced him, in somewhat unsteady letters, as "The Invisible King Ggypt," and beyond that wistful claim his only assets I ever knew of were a large silver belt buckle, a pair of gold-filled Air Force dark glasses then in great demand, and a white girl in Panama named Francesca with whom he accommodated such ranking strays as the likely source of the glasses themselves.

He'd appear in them, and that silver buckle, right after payday; and when his number failed again to turn up in the National Lottery both went back into pawn for another number, until another payday. The lottery was a glimpse of liberation he shared with the whole silver payroll and some of the gold too, alert for signs: The day one of those huge steam cranes on the canal's rim tipped and crashed on the bottom you couldn't find a lottery ticket with the crane's number for sale on any street in Panama.

Murrell's other and far less substantial hope of deliverance lay in his own inspired vision of returning with me to New York as my valet. I could never really convince him that the decision wasn't just a matter of whim on my part, though out there under the stars he seemed as resigned to being canceled out eight hours of the twenty-four for his $18 a week as I was vexed at almost four times the pay for the same proposition.

I finally tried to mitigate it with pages torn from "Hugo's Simplified Spanish" held under the dim light at my controls, but his Spanish was as fluently indifferent as his English and he met any query on elementary Spanish grammar with the same evasive good humor he used to field the origin of The Invisible King Ggypt, to shield my ignorance of machinery and get me through the job. It wasn't a camaraderie that went down well with the gold payroll, and by the time I'd been seen more than once bent to the wrong drinking fountain, riding up from some bolt-sorting job on the canal floor on the wrong elevator, the overhaul was done and it was just as well, and I never saw Murrell again.

I never saw any of those gold-payroll drifters again either. They pulled clean shirts on over their tattoos and packed up with talk of contracts on the Arab pipeline, "Two years ain't long, not if you say it real fast . . . ," and no more concern than they had for the war just coming along next door in Costa Rica, greeting my sudden notion of going up there for it with, "Them girls in San José, they're as white as you are."

The fighting was out around Cartago, where I was handed over to a young captain named Madero and issued a banged-up Springfield that was stolen from me the same day. We leveled an airstrip out there for arms coming in from Guatemala. *Life* magazine showed up and rearranged the cartridge belt for an old French Hotchkiss over the blond sergeant's shoulders before they took his picture beside it, and when the arms came in we celebrated with a bottle of raw cane liquor and the sergeant took us home for dinner where I met the most beautiful girl I've ever seen and passed out at the table. When it was all over I stayed around San José for a while, and I never saw that sergeant's sister Maria Eugenia again, and finally came home on a Honduran banana boat.

I heard somewhere later that Madero, flying one of the army's new planes, was killed when he hit a mountain. Tony Arias is dead, and his brother Roberto crippled by a senseless pistol shot, and I have never gone back. The old Tivoli is gone too; so, for me, is Maria Eugenia who was, in fact, as white as I was, and The Invisible King Ggypt who was not; and at last, isn't even this small self-serving effort to seize it again, to try to hang onto it all, as unrealistic and as futile as our country is trying to hang onto its own lost youth down there? to those days of privilege when we could put a whole nation on the silver payroll and slum in smaller countries' wars, protected for so long, both of us, by everything but history from the sheer remorse of growing up?

THE RUSH FOR SECOND PLACE

PUBLISHED IN THE APRIL 1981 issue of *Harper's Magazine*, this essay was initially titled "Failure" and submitted to *The Wall Street Journal* at the request of Jeffrey Burke, an erstwhile copy editor at *Harper's*. When Burke's plan for a monthly magazine attached to the *Journal* fell through, the manuscript went to *Harper's*—where aside from replacing the phrase "glossy car and whiskey ads" with "television commercials," the editors made only minor changes.

The density of literary references in the finished essay reflects the syllabus of a course Gaddis had taught a few years before at Bard College on the theme of failure in American Literature: Frederick Exley's *A Fan's Notes* ("the 'misfit' in America's value system"); Max Weber's *The Protestant Ethic and the Spirit of Capitalism* ("Puritan and Calvinist teachings as a moral foundation for the emergence of capitalism"); Edward Bellamy's late nineteenth-century utopian novel *Looking Backward*; Upton Sinclair's *The Jungle* ("the nightmare side of the 'survival of the fittest' "); "Dale Carnegie's vulgarized application of pragmatism for gain in *How to Win Friends and Influence People*"; John Holt, *How Children Fail* ("education's false solutions to false values"), Alan Sillitoe's *The Loneliness of the Long Distance Runner*; Doris Kearns on Lyndon Johnson; Myra Friedman on Janis Joplin; Sue Kaufman's *Diary of a Mad Housewife*; A. Alvarez on Sylvia Plath;

and Joan Didion's *Play It As It Lays*, "on the importance of fictions however tawdry in dealing with the ultimate 'nothing.' "

In the course, as in the essay, Gaddis addresses "the challenge that American fiction has centered upon from its beginnings." As he told his students on the first day of class, the writer in America faces an inescapable "predicament": "With no long history and no class system, with the tradition of a complete freedom to do and become what one wants to, we are confronted with essential human problems of what, exactly, is worth doing. And in fiction, this [challenge] takes the shape of 'the way things should be' as opposed to 'the way things are.' We are still I think involved in unraveling what we adopted as a history without a past, a derivation of the Protestant ethic in which a calling to honest work produces good income; good income becomes the goal; and the goal produces good income. This is what I think produced our American philosophy of pragmatism, in which expediency becomes the goal in terms, too often, of the way 'things are,' rather than the way things 'should be.' And this in turn is the confrontation that much of our fiction tries to describe and redress."

THE RUSH FOR SECOND PLACE

Missed Victories in America

Ronald Reagan recalled it with the word "noble," McGeorge Bundy felt that "somewhere, somehow, the United States could have done better," and Alexander Solzhenitsyn saw the whole thing as a pacifist betrayal and a failure of nerve on the part of the American intelligentsia. Gerald Ford, speaking as our unelected president at the moment of that final humiliating withdrawal from Vietnam, chose the metaphor of the game. It seems a shame, he said, "that at the last minute of the last quarter we don't make that special effort. . . . It just makes me sick. . . ."

Ford was, after all, a veteran of the playing fields of Michigan, where he had been voted Most Valuable Player on a college football team that lost every conference game; but these were not the fields where winning mattered less than "how you played the game." They were closer to those of his predecessor, lately mired in Watergate while busy on the phone with strategies for the next day's victory by the Washington Redskins. These were not the fields of Eton, where Waterloo was won, but nearer those of the legendary Vince Lombardi, where "winning is not a sometime thing. It is an all-time thing. You don't win once in a while, you don't do things right once in a while, you do them right all the time. There's no room for second place. There's only one place, and that's first place."

Asking "if a full-fledged America suffered a real defeat from a small communist half-country, how can the West hope to stand firm in the future?" Solzhenitsyn deplored the decline in courage "particularly noticeable among the ruling groups and the intellectual elite, causing an impression of loss of courage by the entire society." He'd descended upon Harvard that gloomy 1978 commencement day from his private gulag in Vermont to bear witness at the outset that "truth seldom is pleasant; it is almost invariably bitter," and went on to regale his audience from the full catalogue of bitter truths he'd managed to unearth about the West in general and America in particular. "Active and tense competition permeates all human thoughts without opening a way to free spiritual development," he cautioned, moving from the deluded pose that humanism declares man born to be happy, to attributing our woes to our delusion of the attainment of happiness through the relentless pursuit of material goods. But "one psychological detail has been overlooked," the novelist confided: "the constant desire to have still more things and a still better life and the struggle to obtain them imprints many Western faces with worry and even depression, though it is customary to conceal such feelings."

Customary or not, Cyril Connolly, visiting New York thirty years before, had had no trouble finding "many traces of this unrest. Insecurity reigns. Almost everyone hates his job . . . books on how to be happy, how to obtain peace of mind, how to win friends and influence people, how to breathe, how to achieve a cheap sentimental humanism at other people's expense, how to become a Chinaman like Lin Yutang and make a lot of money, how to be a Baha'i or breed chickens all sell in the millions."

In fact, that precious "psychological detail" that Solzhenitsyn unveiled for this book-ridden audience could have been overlooked only by overlooking the main body of American literature and the novelists who have been struggling with the bitter truths of conflict and failure in American life since, and well before, he was born.

A generation before that blessed event Edward Bellamy had written, in his utopian novel *Looking Backward*, "For thirty years I had lived among them, and yet I seemed to have never noted before how drawn and anxious were their faces, of the rich as of the poor, the refined, acute faces of the educated as well as the dull masks of the ignorant. And well it might be so, for I saw now, as never before I had seen so plainly, that each as he walked constantly turned to catch the whispers of a specter at his ear, the specter of Uncertainty."

Vince Lombardi's exhortation lives on today in that "wild animal roar," that "outpouring of some visceral, primordial feeling of ascendancy and dominance" in the Astrodome and, decorously framed, on the office walls of middle management—often along with Murphy's law, and, further down the line, "This is a non-profit enterprise, even if we didn't plan it that way." Elsewhere, such doggerel revives as "Everyone told him it couldn't be done; with a will he went right to it. He tackled the thing that couldn't be done, and couldn't do it." A nine-year-old passes in a T-shirt that proclaims, "I can't cope"; test scores drop; classrooms empty and jails fill; alcoholism gains illness status and drugs abound— prescriptions for the middle class, cash for the kids and ghettos; and the day's mail brings flyers offering courses in Mid-life Crisis, Stress Management, Success Through Assertiveness, Reflexology, Shiatsu, Hypnocybernetics, and The Creative You. Books disappear overnight or are instant "best-sellers": mortifying confessionals and est, group therapy, primal screams and "making it," pious plagiaries on moral fiction and Maharishi Mahesh Yogi's TM Technique for reducing blood pressure and increasing self-esteem. Even impotence is briefly chic; the movie screen offers the dreary sentimental humanisms of Woody Allen achieved at the expense of cast and audience alike and, for the beer crowd, *Rocky*. There is a rush for second place.

Bad money drives out good, and Gresham's law accelerates;

but if this is indeed the cheap money we see being spent left and right, where is the good being hoarded? Our highly touted religious revival thrives with enthusiastic custodians. No stranger to private jets, poolside parleys, and expense-account living—his fund-raising efforts reportedly yield $1 million a week—Moral Majority's Reverend Jerry Falwell is among the first to recognize material wealth as "God's way of blessing people who put him first."

Eager to share his spiritual good fortune through the political process, Falwell disdains the constitutional niceties separating church and state as a problem that "isn't violating anything. The problem is that we don't agree with those buzzards—and that we outnumber them." Yet the real problem lies well beyond the Lord's hosts versus the buzzards of secular humanism, or even whether the struggle "to have still more things and a still better life," which Solzhenitsyn so deplores, must stigmatize secular humanism alone as Christianity's common enemy.

The Reformation swept away the intercession of the Roman church in the sixteenth century and posed man's direct accountability to God. We might do worse, then, than to pursue this accountability in an effort to discover what became of it in the form Christianity took in the shaping of America; whether, in fact, the Protestant ethic fostered the very secular humanism it is now being summoned to do battle against and, if this is so, whether it can prevail with half the equation missing.

"I don't think people ever *want* to lose their faith either in religion or anything else," Father Rothschild said gently in 1930 in Evelyn Waugh's *Vile Bodies*. "I know very few young people, but it seems to me that they are all possessed with an almost fatal hunger for permanence. I think all these divorces show that. People aren't content just to muddle along nowadays. . . . My private schoolmaster used to say, 'If a thing's worth doing at all, it's worth doing well.' My Church has taught that in different words for several centuries. But these young people have got hold of another end of the stick, and for all we know it may be the right one. They say, 'If a thing's not worth doing well, it's not worth doing at all.' It makes everything very difficult for them."

"Good heavens," counters Mr. Outrage, "I should think it did. What a darned silly principle. I mean to say, if one didn't do anything that wasn't worth doing well—why, what *would* one do . . . ?"

The half century since has proliferated with an embarrassment of riches. A character in current fiction remarks that there have never been so many opportunities to do so many different things not worth doing; and a society where failure can reside in simply not being a "success" holds its most ignominious defeats in store for those—we call them "losers"—who fail at something that was not worth doing in the first place. In *The Lonely Crowd* David Riesman dwelt on the parent who demands "conformity as evidence of characterological fitness and self-discipline." From the Puritan's anxious search for some assurance of salvation, secularization turns to the status hierarchy. "On the one hand the parent looks for signs of potential failure—this search arises in part from guilty and anxious preoccupation about himself. On the other hand he looks for signs of talent—this must not be wasted."

More pointedly, in the fiction of a generation before, George Babbitt told his daughter, "Now you look here! The first thing you got to understand is that all this uplift and flipflop and settlement-work and recreation is nothing in God's world but the entering wedge for socialism. The sooner a man learns he isn't going to be coddled, and he needn't expect a lot of free grub and, uh, all these free classes and flipflop and doodads for his kids unless he earns 'em, why, the sooner he'll get on the job and produce—produce—produce!" Sinclair Lewis drew Babbitt as a man who "made nothing in particular, neither butter nor shoes nor poetry, but he was nimble in the calling of selling houses for more than people could afford to pay," who "simply can't understand how I ever came to have a pair of shillyshallying children like Rone and Ted."

"Anyway I've got no children myself," Waugh's Mr. Outrage takes up, "and I'm thankful for it. I don't understand them and I don't want to. They had a chance after the war that no generation has ever had. There was a whole civilization to be saved . . . and all they seem to do is to play the fool."

He spoke just a half century ago; and if they did these things in a green tree, what shall be done in the dry?

"A visitor strolling along the Bahnhofstrasse here," read a recent news story datelined Zurich, "gazing into the windows of some of the world's most exclusive shops or pausing outside the headquarters of some of the world's most powerful banks, would be hard put to believe that not too long ago scores of young people paraded naked there, smashing storefronts and shouting imprecations at their horrified elders."

And not just in Zurich but in Bern, in Lausanne, and in Geneva itself, where, four centuries gone, economic conditions "were so bourgeois, and on such a small scale, that Capitalism was able to steal into the Calvinist ethic." This "Protestant ethic of the 'calling,' " continues Ernst Troeltsch, "with its severity and its control of the labour rendered as a sign of the assurance of election, made service in one's 'calling,' the systematic exercise of one's energies, into a service both necessary in itself and appointed by God, in which profit is regarded as the sign of the Divine approval. . . . The owner of wealth or property is 'the Lord's Steward,' and administers a Divine gift which has been entrusted to him."

That was pretty much the way John D. Rockefeller looked at it, and at himself, bringing his talents for organization to America's chaotic oil industry three hundred years later. Here was no idler, no boozer, no skirt-chaser, but a man who saw eye to eye with an ethic that regarded "laziness and idleness as the source of all evil, and the result of a failure to impose discipline," who could feel "the obligation towards property as towards something great, which ought to be maintained and increased for its own sake" and who subscribed to the philosophy articulated in this Sunday school address: "The American Beauty rose can be produced in the splendour and fragrance which bring cheer to its beholder only by sacrificing the early buds which grow up around it. This is not an evil tendency in business. It is merely a working-out of a law of nature and a law of God.

"The growth of a large business," it concluded, "is merely a survival of the fittest." And while it was pointed out elsewhere that all the survival of the fittest meant was that the fittest survive and—the American Beauty rose notwithstanding—that the fittest need not necessarily mean the best, Rockefeller's ethic was widely applauded. In a world where Darwinism had pulled the rug from under the first book of the Bible and appeared, therewith, to threaten Christianity itself, he had synthesized the two without a blink.

"American society saw its own image in the tooth-and-claw version of natural selection," Richard Hofstadter wrote of that century's last decade, "and that its dominant groups were therefore able to dramatize this vision of competition as a thing good in itself," to which William Graham Sumner had already borne witness "that if we do not like the survival of the fittest, we have only one possible alternative, and that is the survival of the unfittest."

At the outset of Upton Sinclair's novel *The Jungle*, where he burst forth in 1906, Jurgis Rudkus vigorously agreed. Scorning the despairing job seekers around him in the Chicago stockyards as "broken-down tramps and good-for-nothings, fellows who have spent all their money drinking, and want to get more for it," this brand newcomer demanded, " 'Do you want me to believe that with these arms'—and he would clench his fists and hold them up in the air, so that you might see the rolling muscles—'that with these arms people will ever let me starve?' " Would they ever! By page 161 (and 180 still to go) "they" had "ground him beneath their heel, they had devoured all his substance; they had murdered his old father, they had broken and wrecked his wife, they had had crushed and cowed his whole family; and now they were through with him. . . . He had no wit to trace back the social crime to its far sources—he could not say that it was the thing men have called 'the system' that was crushing him to the earth. . . ."

It was the earth Jurgis had sprung from, the mud of a Lithuanian farm, to become a disposable item in that gigantic shift from status to contract that swept Western civilization in the burgeoning of the new industrial society. Here, "status" had none of the invidious quality it would later embrace in Babbitt's wish to be known as a "realtor" rather than a real-estate salesman; none of the current obnoxious fulfillment of José Ortega y Gasset's thesis:

"not that the vulgar believes itself super-excellent and not vulgar, but that the vulgar proclaims and imposes the rights of vulgarity, or vulgarity as a right"—the "right" that afflicts us in glossy car and whiskey ads. Quite the opposite: here, status still expressed Martin Luther's translation of the Greek word for "toil" as a "calling." Here, "God accomplishes all things through you," Kemper Fullerton cites; "through you he milks the cow and does the most servile works," conveying "the idea that the proper performance of such a secular task is a religious obligation." Fleeing that outmoded, static world, which held no threat of failure since it had no place for success, Jurgis's immigrant effort to proclaim himself an individual by putting a price on his labors reduced him to simply that, a unit of work without status, without a "calling," and without any authority as an individual whatsoever. In a world increasingly beset by applied scientific principles, by the tangible, the quantifiable, the measurable "useful fact," he had singlehandedly rendered himself just those things.

The year Jurgis was being obliterated in Packingtown, William James, farther east, was picking up the pieces of his earlier speculations at Columbia University. In his lecture "What Pragmatism Means," the pragmatist, said James, "turns away from abstraction and insufficiency, from verbal solutions, from bad *a priori* reasons, from fixed principles, closed systems, and pretended absolutes and origins. He turns towards concreteness and adequacy, towards facts, towards action and towards power. . . . You must," he insisted—bypassing "God" as a verbal solution—"bring out of each word its practical cash-value, set it at work within the stream of your experience."

Pragmatism, says Hofstadter, "was absorbed into the national culture when men were thinking of manipulation and control."

Frederick Winslow Taylor had been thinking on those lines since the eighties and was already busy with the time: motion studies that would launch him as the "father of scientific management." In a nation ravenous for progress in the shape of material goods, the logical outcome was the concept of mass production, the assembly line, the consequent reduction of every element involved to proportions amenable to quantification, manipulation, and control, and inevitably the blossoming of such collateral frights as "human engineering," of such insidious goals as "the engineering of consent."

These elements were the heart, or at least the sinews, of the rise of automation and the development of computer technology, prompting hopes in some quarters for the fulfillment of Lord Keynes's speculations in 1930 "that the day might not be all that far off when everybody would be rich. We shall then," E. F. Schumacher, author of *Small Is Beautiful*, found him saying, "once more value ends above means and prefer the good to the useful. . . . But beware! The time for all this is not yet. For at least another hundred years we must pretend to ourselves and to everyone that fair is foul and foul is fair; for foul is useful and fair is not. Avarice and usury and precaution must be our gods for a little longer still. For only they can lead us out of the tunnel of economic necessity into daylight. . . ."

Put all together in the sixties—from the prosaic quantification of the "body-count" to that chilling light at the end of the tunnel—it would spell Vietnam.

The real marvel in our complex technological world, given the frustration implicit in Murphy's law, is not that if anything can go wrong it will go wrong but that anything goes right at all. In communication and control "we are always," wrote cybernetics' pathfinder Norbert Wiener, "fighting nature's tendency to degrade the organized and to destroy the meaningful." The more complex the message, the greater the chance for error. Entropy rears as a central preoccupation of our time. As computer technology's appetite for precision is enhanced by its own enlarged complexity, the archenemy, disorganization, must look increasingly to human error for an ally; and failing error, where foul is useful and fair is not, to sheer deceit. If Robert McNamara's computers wanted "body counts," they should have them; if the squad leader whose job was billed as fighting for freedom knew his real job was simply to make the man above him look good to the man above *him*, the body count escalated accordingly; and whose bodies were they anyway? V.C.s'? Children's? Old ladies'? Clear fictions?

For McNamara, "the can-do man in the can-do society, in the can-do era," as David Halberstam recommends him, "time was not just money, it was, even more important, action, decisions, cost effectiveness, power." Angry that General Harkins had "seriously misled" him on the progress of the war but not to be outdone, he was on hand with some lies of his own to cloud the evidence on the Tonkin Gulf incident, a casus belli provoked by South Vietnamese PT boat raids conducted with full knowledge and control shared by Harkins, McGeorge Bundy, Dean Rusk, and McNamara himself.

A year later there were 184,000 United States troops fighting an undeclared war in South Vietnam and 385,000 the year following, with the attendant conspiracy to avoid a tax increase by concealing the war's real projected costs for 1967—$6 to $7 billion above the $10 billion acknowledged—from the president's own economic advisors, from Congress, and from the American people.

McGeorge Bundy, busy since 1961 in that quagmire of deceit as special assistant to the president for national security affairs, slipped off to a substantial salary at the Ford Foundation; and McNamara, for whom by 1967 the war had become "a human waste, yes, but it was also no longer cost effective," was off to the World Bank.

But there was still Dean Rusk, dutifully defining the traits instilled in him by a Calvinist father as a "sense of the importance of right and wrong which was something that was before us all the time." And there was still Lyndon Johnson, whose mother's Protestant ethic had left no room for uncontrolled and frivolous behavior, but who'd let him win at childhood games even when it meant changing the rules.

"Deep down I knew—I simply knew—that the American people loved me," he would tell his biographer, Doris Kearns. "After all that I'd done for them and given to them, how could they help but love me? And I knew that it was only a very small percentage that had given up, who had lost faith. We had more than three million young people serving in uniform. . . . They were just there, from daylight to dark fighting for freedom and willing to die for it." Some 30,000 of them, in fact, willing or not, had done just that.

Lyndon Johnson was obviously not a man to settle simply for being liked. He had tried that once with Dean Acheson, who responded bluntly, "You are not a very likable man." In his rising paranoia Johnson was, writ large, that "unprecedented inner loneliness of the single individual" that Max Weber had found at the core of the Protestant ethic, where again, as Fullerton elaborates on Weber's thesis, "since the individual is elected by the eternal decree of God, all intermediaries between God and man are, at least theoretically, excluded. . . . The soul stands in the presence of its God in awful isolation."

This was clearly no John D. Rockefeller, to whom the need for human affection scarcely occurred, prepared as he was at any moment to give a face-to-Face account of his divine steward-ship, until his publicist Ivy Lee let him know he was cordially loathed; who, failing the generation around him, stuffed his pockets with dimes to buy what pals he could in the new one. Nearer Babbitt perhaps, writ small, who "liked to like the people about him; he was dismayed when they did not like him." Safe in the American tradition of the "self-made man," Babbitt could credit himself with a success ascribable only to a system that could in turn embrace "selling houses for more than people could afford to pay" as a "calling." But there was also Babbitt—the content of his theology limited to "a supreme being who had tried to make us perfect, but presumably had failed"—plumbing the shallows of his own inner loneliness, confessing to his son on the novel's last page, "Now, for heaven's sake, don't repeat this to your mother. . . . I've never done a single thing I've wanted to in my whole life!"

For one Robert McNamara who "hated failure," who "had conquered it all his life, risen above it, despised it in others," we can count a million Willy Lomans: "I'll go to Hartford. I'm very well liked in Hartford," he tells his wife in Arthur Miller's *Death of a Salesman*. "You know, the trouble is, Linda, people don't seem to take to me. . . . I gotta overcome it. I know I gotta overcome it. I'm not dressing to advantage, maybe. . . ." He's been on the road for his company for thirty-six years and here, suicide bound, is the dark side of the coin; "created free and equal" in his right to pursue happiness, he is racked by the shame and guilt of failure when the system itself goes sour.

At about the time Lord Keynes opened the Great Depression with his postponement for a century of the day when we might "once more value ends above means and prefer the good to the useful," he was confirmed by the appearance of a disingenuous book filled with recipes for exchanging the remnants of the things worth being for those presumably worth having. A casebook of manipulation, expediency, "what works," *How to Win Friends and Influence People* combined the worst of both possible worlds: pragmatism's "cash value" of an idea and the inner loneliness of the Protestant ethic. There, in the absence of a "calling" and in place of the soul's stance in God's presence "in awful isolation," it has tendered the shabby temporal alternative of "being liked" to more than nine million readers. "Better to go down dignified/With boughten friendship at your side/Than none at all./Provide, provide!" Robert Frost intoned. And Ortega y Gasset posed the "mass-man," who "accepts the stock of commonplaces, prejudices, fag-ends of ideas or simply empty words which chance has piled up within his mind, and with a boldness explicable only by his ingenuousness, is prepared to impose them everywhere." "I may not be any Rockefeller or James J. Shakespeare," says Babbitt, "but I certainly do know my own mind. . . ." And Willy Loman, no Polonius, advises his sons, "The man who makes an appearance in the business world, the man who creates personal interest, is the man who gets ahead. Be liked and you will never want."

"Approval itself," David Riesman writes, "irrespective of content, becomes almost the only unequivocal good in this situation: one makes good when one is approved of." This hunger for approval appears in all its desperate trappings in John Holt's excellent, profoundly saddening book *How Children Fail*. The overriding desire of the children in his elementary classroom to please, irrespective of the lesson's content or even the question itself; the anguished search for an answer, any answer, even the wrong one, to end the anxiety; and the hapless attempts to manipulate his authority, later drove him to recommend the disbanding of schools altogether. But finally he came round: these schools were, after all, preparing these children for exactly the contentless, need-for-approval, manipulative society he saw out there waiting for them.

"I've had twenty or thirty kinds of jobs since I left home," Willy Loman's son Biff, the onetime high school football star, tells his brother. "I'm thirty-four years old, I oughta be makin' my future. That's when I come running home. And now, I get here, and I don't know what to do with myself. I've always made a point of not wasting my life, and everytime I come back here I know that all I've done is to waste my life."

"I mean to say," says Mr. Outrage, "if one didn't do anything that wasn't worth doing well—why, what *would* one do?"

Possibly introduce a new cultural style: "Call it psychedelic, or call it, as its own protagonists have, a 'counter-culture,' " wrote Harvard sociologist Daniel Bell, dismissing the sixties as the decade closed as "simply an extension of the hedonism of the 1950s. . . . Just as the political radicalism of the 1960s followed the failure of political liberalism the decade before, so the psychedelic extremes—in sexuality, nudity, perversions, pot, and rock—

and the counter-culture followed on the forced hedonism of the 1950s." No mention here, in the entire passage, in fact, of Watts, Newark, Detroit, of the shootings, burning, rioting, the assassinations, the 543,000 United States troops in South Vietnam and the 130,000 American casualties dead, maimed, and missing. Rather, Bell determines, "The counter-culture proved to be a conceit. It was an effort, largely a product of the youth movement, to transform a liberal life-style into a world of immediate gratification and exhibitionistic display. In the end, it produced little culture and countered nothing."

"I don't understand them, and I don't want to," Mr. Outrage echoes. "There was a whole civilization to be saved and remade— and all they seem to do is to play the fool."

In fact, the "heroes of the Sixties were losers who survived or martyrs," Doris Kearns observes. "The cult of failure spread. As Benjamin Braddock in *The Graduate*, Dustin Hoffman came to epitomize the unknown everyman who was the hero of the late Sixties: uncertain, alienated, and, by any traditional standards, a loser." And more than that he was, in many ways, a pale version of the real cult hero of the fifties: James Dean portraying youth's desperate, inarticulate appeal to a father—willfully opaque in *East of Eden*, helpless in *Rebel Without a Cause*—for a direct answer, for some measure of accountability, for something, anything, on which to base some hope for its own worth. It was a despairing version of the demand for honesty, the seizure of *being* honest, presented fiercely in Alan Sillitoe's *The Loneliness of the Long Distance Runner*, poignantly in *The Catcher in the Rye*, triumphantly in *Huckleberry Finn*.

It was in Biff Loman's cry, "Pop! I'm a dime a dozen, and so are you . . . ! I'm nothing! I'm nothing, Pop. Can't you understand that? There's no spite in it any more. I'm just what I am, that's all."

It was in Fred Exley's "fictional memoir" of his father, a reduced small-town sports hero, in the self-abnegation in his worship of the college-turned-professional football star, where his readers found themselves with him suddenly wanting to shout, "Listen, you son of a bitch, life isn't all a goddam football game! You won't always get the girl! Life is rejection and pain and loss. . . ." *A Fan's Notes* closed out the sixties after Exley had reread and burned an earlier draft he'd spent a year writing, "because on every page I had discovered I loathed the America I knew."

And it was in a German novel from a generation before that was being read, imitated, and discussed, with the eternal question presenting itself: "whether all this was simple stupidity and human frailty, a common depravity, or whether this sentimental egoism and perversity, this slovenliness and two-facedness of feeling was merely a personal idiosyncrasy of the Steppenwolves. And if this nastiness was common to men in general, I could rebound from it with renewed energy into hatred of all the world, but if it was a personal frailty, it was good occasion for an orgy of hatred of myself."

The newspapers of 1973 headlined Richard Nixon's second-term inauguration, the ceasefire in Vietnam the next day, Lyndon Johnson's fatal heart attack the day after, and eventually, one of them, SUICIDE: SECOND LEADING CAUSE OF DEATH AMONG PEOPLE 15 TO 24. The information: "More girls attempt suicide but more boys succeed. One reason advanced for this is that the methods generally used by girls (razor and pills) are less certain than the methods usually chosen by boys (guns and hanging)." And the psychologist's attribution: "an inability to communicate, and a feeling of isolation and loneliness, as the 'most overwhelming' contributing factors to young suicides, of whom fewer than 30 percent leave notes."

Lyndon Johnson's heroes were winners: Andrew Jackson, Franklin D. Roosevelt, "Lucky" Lindbergh. By contrast, the late Ivan Morris wrote of another type of hero, in the complex Japanese tradition, who "represents the very antithesis of an ethos of accomplishment. He is the man whose single-minded sincerity will not allow him to make the manoeuvres and compromises that are so often needed for mundane success. . . . He is wedded to the losing side and will ineluctably be cast down. Flinging himself after his painful destiny, he defies the dictates of convention and common sense, until eventually he is worsted by his enemy, the 'successful survivor.' . . . Faced with defeat, the hero will typically take his own life in order to avoid the indignity of capture, vindicate his honour, and make a final assertion of his sincerity."

It is, in effect, a final assertion of accountability. Here at home, on the other hand, where suicide is a sin, a crime, a confession of failure, or at least a desperate avoidance of failure, we have only "successful survivors."

"Large and painful events, unless they are closely studied, have a habit of teaching us the wrong lessons," McGeorge Bundy announced in a 1975 commencement address at the University of Texas in Austin, when the echoes of the last hurrahs (in Vietnamese) had barely begun to fade in Saigon. He had come there to deplore "the immense cost of a breakdown in relations between the president and Congress." Not denying, he said, the "extraordinary difficulty of maintaining effective connection with a Congress which has largely lost its own traditional trust in relevant committees and visible leaders, one must remark that a self-defeating predilection both for secrecy and for personalism has marked the recent conduct of our diplomacy."

With the disclaimer that this might not be the place or the time "to examine the shallow pretense that the people and the Congress really knew about it at the time," was this to be a close study of that "large and painful event," a candid unraveling of the secrecy, the personalism, the shallow pretenses to the people and to Congress that had crowded the administrations he had served in the sixties?

Not likely. Not in Austin.

That decade he blithely consigned to history, where "probably no administration or Congress over the last twenty years will be held harmless. . . ." He was here to nail the "successful survivors" of the following administration with "the most dramatic episode of all": President Nixon's sweeping assurance to President Thieu that United States forces "would not stand idly by in the event of renewed large-scale military action by Hanoi," made without Congress's knowledge, precluding Gerald Ford's winning try in the last minute of the last quarter. As though "winning" would have ended it.

Given Nixon's predilection for theatrics, that may, of course, qualify as far more dramatic than the backstage budget deceits and taxation avoidance of the sixties that launched the inflation we are still enjoying today. As a man without a center, one whose Quaker past rose only to shore up early poverty and tear-streamed demonstrations of a manipulative sincerity incapable of any ethical or moral grasp, Nixon might represent the most "successful survivor" of them all, bar one.

Henry Kissinger, kneeling beside him in prayer some four years and some 20,000 American deaths after their mandate to end that still-undeclared war in Vietnam, had absorbed "the manoeuvres and compromises that are so often needed for mundane success" well outside the American tradition. Like Metternich, whose manipulative, secretive politics had made him Europe's chief arbiter in the early nineteenth century, Kissinger worked hard to be made a prince by the second act. Now, in the third, he lurks in the wings, carrying "a lot of baggage," and the labels—Chile, Angola, Iran, the Middle East commute, Vietnam, Cambodia, Laos—are a hodgepodge of manipulative failures, and yet . . .

And yet, as William Pfaff pointed out succinctly, "He presents himself as a success. He projects success. He is taken as a success. He is talked about for high office once again. It is a striking case of style over substance. It is an American success story."

Haunted five years later by those triumphant front-page grins of Kissinger and Gerald Ford over the thrilling rescue of the merchant ship *Mayaguez* and its crew of thirty-nine, with United States losses at only thirty-eight, could Jimmy Carter be faulted for seizing second place, calling his aborted rescue mission of the hostages in Iran at a cost of a mere eight an "incomplete success"?

Just halfway through Lord Keynes's century it is all, somehow, an American success story.

Following failure so massive as to threaten an underpinning of the entire economy, Chrysler's rush for second place is precipitate. Bellwether of free enterprise, it abruptly confronts the taxpayers' ravaged good faith, tin cup in hand, its six-figure-salaried successful survivors accountable not, of course, to the taxpayers but to its stockholders. Elsewhere the papers and the courts seethe with cases calling people, officials, corporations, law enforcers, and the laws themselves to account, and occasionally someone gets enough time in prison to write a highly profitable book about it. Organized crime, where successful survivors are few, lists CIA consultations on the art of assassination high in its résumé and poses as the model of efficiency. Deftly cornering second place, the FBI precludes failure with its Abscam program, in which the crime—duly arranged and recorded—is solved before it is committed, netting, among others, Congressman Richard Kelly, already called to account by Christian Voice for his votes on "fourteen key moral issues" where he'd scored 100 percent. Even the highways mirror bewilderment over accountability to absolutes, and to their temporal watchdogs, in bumper stickers reading *Keep God in America*, as though He were, this very moment, making good His escape down I-95, scorning Ortega's counsel that "it is precisely because man's vital time is limited, precisely because he is mortal, that he needs to triumph over distance and delay. For an immortal being, the motorcar would have no meaning."

"Thus we mix good and evil, right and wrong and make space for the absolute triumph of absolute Evil in the world," Solzhenitsyn preached that gloomy day in Cambridge, managing to pose absolute Good only in the most amorphous terms and therefore scarcely absolute; able, in fact, to pose Evil's absolute in no more satisfactory terms than those of his own flawed, temporal enemy. And mounted against that enemy—billions upon billions of dollars and nine years hence at best—if the vast Bugs Bunny concept of the MX missile launching system actually comes into being, and someone drops a wrench into its innards, an error into its computers, or an item of "disinformation"—a simple lie will probably do—will anyone be left to sing the day's hit song, "Yes, We Have No Mañanas"? Will anyone have been accountable? And will it, any of it, have been worth doing well?

J R UP TO DATE

A VERSION OF THIS ESSAY NARRATIVE appeared in *The New York Times Book Review* not long after the October stock market crash of 1987; it was titled "Trickle Up Economics: J R Goes to Washington" and cut significantly from the manuscript, which Gaddis titled "*J R* Up to Date." A headnote by Gaddis explained:

> The original "J R" burst on the scene in a novel in 1975, an unkempt 11 year old whose penny stock and defaulted bond operations blossomed into a vast and perilous financial empire through his simple creed of "get all you can" by obeying the letter of the law and evading its spirit at every turn. What has become of him in the 12 years since? The scene is a recent Congressional hearing on the Federal budget.

After yet another fifteen years, the names and references are no longer "up to date," although the economic and political realities haven't changed much: the replacement of manufacturing jobs by low-paying jobs in the U.S. service sector continues; income disparities in the U.S. have only widened further; the Strategic Defense Initiative is back on the table, and J R's slash-and-burn policies—presented not entirely without sympathy by Gaddis—still rule the day. The "ripple effect" noted by the twenty-three-year-old J R extends to current technologies: "all this here software which degenerates all this more software." In short, the novel *J R* is no less up to date in the year 2002 than it was prescient at its publication in 1975, and the boy himself—pushing forty at this printing—has not lost his competitive edge. So we may reinstate the manuscript title without fear that it, too, will look dated—not for some time yet.

Despite Gaddis's explanation, the piece appeared in the *Times* accompanied by the picture of a young cowboy—the illustrator having evidently associated the name with J. R. Ewing of *Dallas*, perhaps the most popular TV show in America at the time.

J R UP TO DATE

—In the absence of the Director of the White House Office of Management and Budget who is occupied with ahm, who is at the Government facility at Allenwood writing his memoirs, we are fortunate in having before us, his Deputy Assistant in the overall policy area Mister J R Van . . .

—Excuse me Mister Chairman, could I make a state . . .

—Now I am pleased to recognize our ranking Republican member, Mister Pecci.

—Thank you Mister Chairman. In view of the momentous task before this committee, let us proceed directly to matters at hand. As a former president of our great nation once observed, when many people are out of work, unemployment results. In this area of vital concern to the American people let me cite an article in a current news magazine, which states that Administration policy advocates, I quote, "carelessness, sloppiness, and widespread incompetence in general on the part of management and workforce alike, are essential to sustaining our economy in these difficult times." I should like the witness to share with us the benefit of his thinking on this matter.

—Okay that's what I, see the overall policy we advocate in this here area is that we advocate full employment.

—Then I'm correct in finding these liberal press allegations without foundation, and that of course in the great American tradition of competetive skills in the free marketplace . . .

—No but see that's exackly what I don't mean, let me collaborate on that a second okay? See how it works is we have what we call this here ripple effect which . . .

—Mister Chairman? May I interrupt the witness to point out that this same article notes that we have the poorest literacy record of all the industrial nations, that 29 million adults can't read a newspaper headline, a third don't know when Columbus landed and . . .

—Okay look Mister Congressman that's just what I'm coming to. Like you start off with all these here schoolteachers? I mean right at the start they were always getting paid worse than anybody, so they were mostly these ladies, right? So you create this second class profession you get second-class people, so now you get all these pupils which can't hardly read so they have these here remedial reading programs. See if these teachers got it right in the first place then all these remedial teachers would be out of work which that's what we call this here ripple effect, where each new job creates like three more new ones. Like half the teachers will retire this next six years and they figure the replacements will be off the real bottom of the academic ladder, so each new one should degenerate like maybe five remedial ones, that's how it works. I mean this last five years of this here Administration the economy has degenerated like 13.5 million new jobs, so . . .

—May I point out to the witness that two million well-paying manufacturing jobs have also been lost, and that most of these new jobs have been generated in the low-paying service sector, half of them below the poverty line where 40 percent of New York City's children live.

—No but wait a second, the . . .

—And since the witness has introduced the area of education, I believe the American people may be interested in learning the credentials of someone so young, holding so high an Administration policymaking post, and I might add whose use of the language suggests some remedial . . .

—No now wait a second, I mean where last year all these PACs handed you guys like $130 million to get elected to Congress so you can help them out, some of us which want to serve the American people can't hardly afford to get elected in this here great democratic process so we have to get appointed. See so anyway all these people which can't read the newspaper and these forty poor children in New York, like if they're going into this service sector you don't have to know when Columbus discovered America to be a busboy, right? Because where they're making this lousy salary they don't hardly pay any taxes anyway, so mainly we're concentrating on these hardworking Americans which are shouldering the tax burden for everybody else, like as you take all these lawyers? I mean over at Japan they have like one lawyer for every twenty thousand people, only here we have one for every five hundred where they all need work, right? So like you're getting this divorce where this first lawyer screws up and quits so you pay him and get this second one which is giving away everything you've got only you have to pay anyway before you get this third one, I mean that's what they call legal ethics right? Like these doctors where you have to get a second opinion because this last ten years these medical malpractice awards went up 835 percent, so these doctors and lawyers are helping each other out, I mean like if the first one got it right who needs a . . .

—I must caution the witness to ahm, to single out these fine professions is hardly the purpose of this hearing, and . . .

—Okay then look Mister Chairman, you take these cars. I mean already this year like eight million have been recalled? Like where Ford just recalled four million where some loose coupling was making the engines catch on fire? I mean if they got it right in the first place here's all these auto parts makers and dealers and repair shops out selling pencils, so this last ten years these product liability lawsuits went up 1,000 percent or you'd have all these lawyers and insurance companies and car makers out in this here service sector taking in each other's laundry, so anyway . . .

—Mister Chairman, I think we might proceed on to other aspects of the . . .

—Right. I mean where you get this here ripple effect really going we can proceed on to the Defense Department, and like I'm not even talking about these double billings and cost overruns and $600 ashtrays which that's just how it all works with these built in incentives, or it wouldn't work at all. See at this here point in time there's like 30,000 companies in military production where the military signs 52,000 contracts every day, so . . .

—The gentleman from California? State your inquiry.

—We were discussing unemployment Mister Chairman, and the witness is straying into the sensitive area of defense procurement. May I suggest certain priorities which do not necessitate targeting that patriotic segment of the economy devoted to serving the American people in its unparalleled effort to . . .

—No now wait a second Mister Congressman that's exackly what I'm talking about, these here priorities. See you take these old historical times like at Rome and all which had these armies and navies which went out and conquered all these foreigners so they could make them pay all these taxes to support everybody at home, right? where they could just hang around in these here togas and talk about philosophy and all? So now it's exackly backwards. Now everybody at home has to work to support the military. I mean that's what these here taxes are mainly all about which we've got this biggest military budget in history where we're not even having a war yet, so the Pentagon wants like $1.8 trillion over this next five years I mean where will they get it? See so that's these priorities where you cut out all this big government spending so this tax money can go where they need it. Like you take this $336 million for medical care and housing for all these here veterans left over from the last war, only we're talking about the next one, so for the same money you get to buy 220 Phoenix air-to-air missiles, right? See mainly these here spending cuts we're proposing like one third of them come from these here low income programs which aren't hardly cost effective taxwise like this $1.5 billion for housing and all for these here elderly and handicapped and this energy assistance for all these here poor people, so for that money you get to buy this whole brand-new Marine anphibious assault ship. Or like you take some big ticket item like this $28 billion B-1 bomber program, so I mean in just one year you cut out these here inflation adjustments for Social Security where all these old people are piling up on us? and these here Federal housing and farming income subsidies? So you're like saving almost the whole cost of it right there. Or you figure just in 1985 where we spent $75.9 billion on Medicare and this other $25 billion on Medicaid, these reforms we're proposing in these here programs should save like $90 billion this next five years where you'd get the B-1 and these 110 MX Peacekeeper warhead missiles where half of them are in silos and the rest are riding around on these here train cars, with enough left over to buy a bunch of these here little single nuculer warhead Midgetmans which . . .

—Mister Chairman? I should like to get back to square one, and we might observe in passing that in seventeen recent MX missile tests only five were equipped with production model guidance systems, and of those five only three hit within the target zone, and so . . .

—No but Mister Congressman we're still on square one, I mean that's exackly this here ripple effect where they're fixing it up, right? Like this here B-1 bomber which it's forty tons overweight so it shakes all over and couldn't hardly hit its target even if it gets there which they're not sure of that too. See how it works is you get all these here used generals and admirals which we pay these big pensions where they retire up a grade where they're used to these free haircuts and doctors and all, so they join these here big defense contractors to help think up these new projects for how to spend this here $300 million a day with these old buddies which are still stuck at the Pentagon, right? So they figure up like this here Bradley anphibious troop vehicle with these here tests like it's Sunday afternoon driving where it can't hardly get through a mud puddle, and like where the Justice Department just dropped fraud charges for these here millions of dollars in these cost overruns on this Sergeant York gun where they spent $1.8 billion on development and scrapped the whole thing because it couldn't hit a barn? And where like 30 percent of these here cruise missile test flights failed? I mean we're talking about full employment which that's where this here ripple effect goes all over the place where this one new project like creates all these new jobs which degenerate like a hundred new ones just trying to rescue it. Like you take that whole NASA thing where this here Challenger blows up because somebody got these here O-rings wrong? So then these audits show where these here millions of dollars just got stolen or lost someplace and these hundreds of millions in these inflated expenses where the . . .

—Mister Pecci? State your inquiry.

—I must object to the witness's prolonged emphasis on the occasional lapses and unforeseen difficulties encountered by the Defense Department in its momentous task of safeguarding the American people, and his failure to mention those who have come forward to cooperate in the Department's ongoing corrective efforts by testifying to occasional departures from procurement practice wherein . . .

—No but holy, I mean that's exackly what I'm doing: I mean these here whistle-blowers you think somebody wants to hire them after they blew this here whistle? Like their job is what's anybody's real job, which is making this guy above him look good to the guy above him like right up to the top, right? So I mean who wants these here whistle-blowers screwing everything up before it even happens, where you cancel out this whole ripple effect and throw everybody out of work? So look. I mean here's this here whole SDI thing where they figure like six bil, wait where's the dot, I mean $60 billion to deploy it by 1994 if we're all still around then, right? I mean where all these very top scientists are saying it won't work even if it works? See so where way back in 1984 they had like five thousand engineers and scientists which this year should go to twenty thousand so like finally you're going to get like six times as many of them per every billion dollars you get in regular industry. So where they're figuring out how they're going to figure out all this here software which degenerates all this more software, you'll get this here ripple effect going where you're going to get a lot more than a couple of busted O-rings. I mean each of these here twenty thousand new jobs will degenerate like fifty new ones just cleaning things up, okay?

—Yes well ahm, yes not exactly okay and may I interrupt the witness to observe that the approach he has presented so eloquently might serve as a recipe for a return to double-digit inflation?

—Sure. It should be right back up there in a couple of years.

—Perhaps the witness has misunderstood the question. And we may note further that when this Administration took office the Federal deficit was $914 billion. This past August it stood at $2.3 trillion. Further, household debt last year reached $2.61 trillion, with a further 9 percent rise predicted for . . .

—Okay look, see what happened was where we tried out this here trickle down theory only it didn't work out so good, I mean it all like got stuck at the top where fifteen years ago this richest 1 percent of the nation held 27 percent of the wealth and now it's almost 36 percent, I mean it mostly like trickled up. And see where the Administration goal was to end inflation it worked so good that this sudden massive collapse of it brought these terrific budget deficits so like now we're this world's biggest debtor nation where if these here Japanese weren't like buying $60 billion in Treasury bonds a year we couldn't hardly pay the gas bill, right?

—We might observe that these bonds represent future obligations of massive proportions, and in fact . . .

—Right, so I mean how can anybody pay back anybody except you get back this high inflation with all these here cheap dollars?

—And in fact, reviewing the overall thrust of the witness's testimony, it might even appear that while we are expending vast sums to arm the nation against the Russians, we are selling it to the Japanese. Now, the gentleman from . . .

—Mister Chairman, I think I'm going to be ill.

—I would entertain the motion that we stand in recess. We wish to thank the witness for his warm and forthright assistance in helping us to clarify Administration policy in these areas touching upon the lives of every single American, and hope he will be able to return to share his thoughts with us on such further matters as our $160 billion trade deficit, if that is agreeable.

—Sure, any time Mister Chairman. I mean we'll burn those bridges when we come to them, right?

AN INSTINCT FOR THE
DANGEROUS WIFE

SHORTLY AFTER THIS REVIEW of Saul Bellow's novel appeared in *The New York Times Book Review* (May 24, 1987), Gaddis sent his son, Matthew, for his "amusement" what was "in effect the 'anatomy of a book review' & why I hope never (cannot afford) to be talked into doing another—most of it obviously my own ('unprofessional') fault, material notes & reading as though preparing for a dissertation on Bellow's work, done I suppose as I would wish for my own work (v. Lehmann Haupt who *reviewed* J R and 10 years later reviewing Carpenter's Gothic said he'd *not read* [the real 'professional'] J R—to say nothing of John Gardner?)." Gardner had reviewed *J R* in *The New York Review of Books* on June 10, 1976.

Clipped to the manuscript and pages of notes on Bellow was the paycheck from the *Times* made out to Gaddis for the review entitled "More Die of Heart Attack." Here as elsewhere, the essay has been checked against the manuscript to restore cuts.

AN INSTINCT FOR THE DANGEROUS WIFE

"Every life has its basic, characteristic difficulty," says middle-aged Benn Crader, contemplating the summing up in a "pain schedule" with endless categories: arthritis, injured vanity, betrayal, injustice, but "the hardest items of all have to do with love. The question then is: So why does everybody persist? If love cuts them up so much, and you see the ravages everywhere, why not be sensible and sign off early?"

"Because of immortal longings" responds his nephew Kenneth, who at thirty-five is still filled with them. "Or just hoping for a lucky break," having yet to encounter one himself.

Disoriented by sexual shocks and mishaps in his fifteen years as a widower, Uncle Benn, a world-famous botanist specializing in lichens, has just taken a wife some twenty years younger, a beauty but more of a torment, "the only child of rich parents, and Balzac very specifically tells you that only children born to wealth make dangerous wives," Kenneth notes in one of his documented indictments. He is stung by his uncle's marriage carried out without his knowledge, or nearer the point without his permission, "still sore because he cheated on me—broke the rules of our relationship." The exploration of this relationship, with its widening ripples of betrayal, deceit and self-deceit, of conspiracy, of sex confused with love and, inevitably, money as stakes in a bruising confidence game, is the material of Saul Bellow's brilliant new novel.

In *More Die of Heartbreak* we welcome back the calamitous wit of *The Adventures of Augie March* and *Herzog* among people diligently struggling to rearrange one another's lives in their efforts to rescue, or simply to define their own, the human comedy implicit in Lenin's poser: Who uses whom? We hear their voices pour from the pages engulfing a plot which is comparatively simple, or would be if left to itself, a possibility that this embattled narrator never entertains for a moment. He is Kenneth Trachtenberg, raised in Paris, his father long since from Valparaiso, Indiana, and thoroughly Europeanized, thriving in the rue Bonaparte as host to literary and intellectual lights including Kenneth's first mentor in Russian studies, Yermelov, on chatting terms with Malraux and Sartre, an accomplished dancer, "Waltz, rumba, conga, tango—when he opened his arms to a woman she could feel that she had come home," an embrace so often rewarded that Kenneth's mother is now ministering to real human misery in Somaliland. "My father is simply fine," he confides under the weight of the "phallic cross" he still carries. "I'm the one with the damages." As a specialist in Russian studies at his uncle's university in that Midwest provincial capital his father had fled, he has come with his "soul in the making" to form "a genuine, I'd say a devouring, friendship" with Uncle Benn.

It is a youthful book. Discussing Tolstoy's difficulties with his character Nekhlyudov in *Resurrection*, the biographer Henri Troyat observes "the gap between protagonist and author has widened with age. The writer has put the ideas of a solitary thinker of seventy-two into the head of a hale and hearty man of thirty-five." Mr. Bellow's success in closing the gap of this same disparity in age is a triumph of his consummate skill as a novelist. But then Kenneth Trachtenberg is hardly hale and hearty, by his own account quite the other way: "a man-sized monkey wrench," hearing impaired, lacking "the sort of character that requires so much height, and this discrepancy has made me a diffident person." Self-absorbed, self-denigrating, self-doubting and the more severely judgmental especially of his elders, he is youth in many of its more impassioned and discomfiting aspects; but the currency of his ideas and his flashes of wit in presenting them, his wide ranging information fused into knowledge, "Locke to Freud with stops at local stations like Bentham and Kierkegaard," Swedenborg, Blake, Blok and Bely, leave no question that these ideas processed for their uses by other minds become his own once he spells them out, finding no reason for existing "unless you made your life a turning point." Ideas flood the book.

"I recommend to everybody [Kenneth never hesitates to recommend] Admiral Byrd's memoirs," he says at the outset. He read the book "because Uncle Benn, who had been in the Antarctic, insisted. Commenting on people isolated in small groups during the long polar night, Byrd says that under such conditions it didn't take them long to find each other out. 'There is no escape anywhere. You are hemmed in on every side by your inadequacies . . .' So in the coldest cold on the face of the earth, X-rays are struck off, showing in gray and white the deformities and diseases of civilized personalities and your own are at the center."

The frozen image—this "image of ice" deposited with Kenneth back in Paris by his teacher Yermelov as "a glacier in the bosom demanding to be thawed"—persists: in Matthew Arnold at thirty finding "his heart was two thirds iced over"; in the frozen subhuman existence of life in the Soviet forced labor camp at Kolyma; in his own academic specialty, St. Petersburg 1913, "the satanic darkness, the abyss of the Antichrist, the horrible islands of gloom, granite and ice, the approaching Terrible Judgment, the crimes of Immanuel Kant against human consciousness, and all the rest of that" to a point where even Uncle Benn's own specialty—the Arctic lichen spending 95 percent of its existence in solid ice, perking up as soon as the sun shines, growing an inch in twenty years millennium after millennium—surfaces in Kenneth's mind as "the little glaciers in civilized breasts," emerging as a kind of totem in their devouring friendship, in Benn's "scrutiny of secret things—total absorption in their hidden design." A man "wrapped in nature. The whole vegetable kingdom was his garment." Benn is made to order for the purposes of his new wife and her father, Dr. Layamon.

Mr. Bellow's novels have always shown a sure instinct for the confidence game, the con man, the promoter, an instinct often colored with affection not unlike Gogol's for Chichikov mortgaging his *Dead Souls.* We have Thaxter in *Humboldt's Gift* blithely signing Charlie Citrine up for the cultural Baedeker of Europe ("Your name will pull down an advance of two hundred and fifty thousand. We split it two ways . . ."); the chaotic Cantabile ("You need somebody tough and practical to handle things for you. I've given this a lot of thought . . ."); finally, in its own cockeyed way, even the gift itself, a film scenario so egregiously awful that its success is practically guaranteed. Mr. Sammler is promoted by the inept enthusiast Feffer while his nephew Wallace is out promoting everything else. Tommy Wilhelm is hustled into lard futures by the seedy Dr. Tamkin, whose byword is *Seize the Day.* But there is nothing blithe, inept or seedy about Dr. Layamon, his patients and pals the big-time developers, powerbrokers, greenmail raiders, his fortune a piece of the action here, a percentage point there. No affection either in the author's portrayal of Doctor's crude demonstrations of his total contempt for women, and the product he's promoting, his only child Matilda who "can be a real bitch, but her bitchiness will be working *for* you . . . great with brilliant people and she can invite them because of you, a big name in your field. The first time they'll come because of you, and afterwards because of her. It's not that you're so antisocial, but a man who likes people doesn't wind up in the Antarctic."

The unsuitable wife, as the critic Frederick R. Karl observes, is "a given in Bellow," his protagonist a man with "an infallible instinct to marry unsuitable women . . . always poised to bring him down as soon as he shows a fault," and an element that remains "constant in Bellow's fiction, after its locus: women are always the cause of man's death, be it spiritual or physical." Eros and Thanatos, the deep-thighed Renata of *Humboldt's Gift*—a big prize apple raised by her mother "under scientific conditions . . . hell-bent on cashing in while she's still in her prime"—solves it handily by leaving Charlie Citrine behind and marrying a wealthy mortician. Old foes with new faces, and here Uncle Benn confronts them again taking refuge in marriage from the demon of sexuality as the husband Matilda Layamon has chosen "to lie on her body," with her father bound to see that he pays the price for the privilege: "If you're going to share the bed of this delicious girl of high breeding and wallow in it, you'll have to find the money it takes. And it so happens that the single most valuable piece of real estate in this town was your property until five years ago when you were screwed out of it, chum. We think you can be made whole."

The scheme for Uncle Benn's redemption—a little blackmail, political arm-twisting, routine betrayals—is simply Doctor Layamon's smooth updating of an earlier generation's brutal venality lingering on in the octogenarian husk of Benn's own uncle, Harold Vilitzer, a.k.a. the Big Heat (said to have once cracked a man's head in a vise), an old-time pol and ward boss as crooked as they came. More recently, Vilitzer has been the architect of a family swindle involving that piece of prize real estate and provoking a failed law suit against him by Benn and his sister, Kenneth's mother, that chewed up the thousands they'd made seeking the millions they'd been "screwed out of." With the Justice Department finally about to descend on Vilitzer and his bought judge, Doctor exhorts Benn's connivance in making his daughter rich without costing himself a penny. "You're entitled to live in style, a rich scientist and not just a research rat." The scene Doctor Layamon and his daughter have in mind is a vacant apartment willed to her by a wealthy aunt called the Roanoke, bourgeois baroque 1910, the feel of a Venetian palace in its spread of chandeliers and a living room the size of a sheep pasture. The Roanoke is, in effect, the third party to the marriage, demanding a fortune to refurbish and maintain it for the scale of entertaining they envisage in guest lists proclaiming the level of their vulgar aspirations in being graced by Dr. Henry Kissinger. "What a girl you married, hey?"

Willful, moody, with a brilliant mind and "more degrees than a thermometer," there is still something disturbing about Matilda's beauty, something "kind of two-dimensional" about the shoulders that reminds Benn of her father. Even in sleep, a demiurge lies hidden under the skin wrapped in her silk and down comforter where "like a sheaf of ferns, there were exhalations of duplicity in that delicate, straight nose." Having elsewhere cited "useful elucidation" among his weaknesses, Kenneth submits "A beautiful woman unites herself with a world-famous botanist. He may think it will serve *his* needs. No, all the while she has been thinking what she can do with *him*." With all of Kenneth's compassion for his uncle, there is a sting in it. Bad enough that Benn had betrayed their relationship; but in youth's ultimate indictment, by assisting at "the degradation of love" Benn has betrayed himself, wandering the Layamons' penthouse dressed in custom tweeds from Doctor's tailor, that "plant observatory, his head" done by a hairstylist. Outside looms the specter of the huge skyscraper risen on that swindled piece of real estate, drawing closer at night in a mass of lighted windows "bigger than the *Titanic*, and the fiery masts like a sign to the children of Israel," bearing down on him sick with "repulsive gratitude to the Layamons for letting him be one of them, choking on lies, accusing himself before God, crying out 'What have I done! Why am I here!' "

One turns the last pages of *More Die of Heartbreak* feeling that no image has been left unexplored by a mind not only at constant work but standing outside itself, mercilessly examining the workings, tracking the leading issues of our times and the composite man in an age of hybrids. The long polar night offers a sharp image for this and indeed any well-wrought novel in its claim as art, isolating people in small groups hemmed in on every side by their inadequacies where they are bound to find each other out, which is fundamentally the task of the novel. Here, in Kenneth's diagnosis, "What it comes down to is that men and women are determined to get out of one another (or tear out) what is simply not to be gotten by any means," proof in their last futile approach to old Vilitzer when Kenneth tells his Uncle Benn "You *can* love a man without loving what he did to you"—that love, like money, is probably best kept in the family.

EREWHON AND THE CONTRACT
WITH AMERICA

PART OF A "SERIES OF ESSAYS by distinguished writers about authors, books, and literary work they passionately believe are ripe for rediscovery," this piece originally appeared in the March 15, 1995 *New York Times Book Review*. In the meantime the "recently elected governor of Texas" referred to in the piece has become president after a contested election, and he has appointed the "Republican senator from Missouri," John Ashcroft, to the position of Attorney General.

EREWHON AND THE CONTRACT
WITH AMERICA

First greeted with a gasp of recognition and haunted by a sense of *déjà vu*, whence came this agenda for "renewing American civilization" that sent some 350 Republicans streaming up the Capitol steps to sign on for their Contract With America? Certain I had visited that fountainhead myself, still nowhere in memory could I recover that marvelous land where morality and good citizenship resided in health and wealth, where poverty and disease were criminal offenses and dishonesty and mendacity in high places treated as mere misfortunes, and I had at last given up the search when, in that morning ritual of despair whose every path of memory leads only to nowhere, NOWHERE . . . suddenly the word flashed across the shaving mirror as the letters in garbled reversal fell neatly into place, and I stood once more at that very New Zealand mountain pass where Samuel Butler's intrepid hero descended a century ago to behold "many a town and city; with buildings that had lofty steeples and rounded domes" rising from the plains of Erewhon.

The most cursory rereading of Butler's utopian fiction of 1872 must, in fact, leave us with little doubt but that "Erewhon" has provided the guidelines for the "opportunity society" of conformity and evasion envisioned by our new Republican majority in the Congress, dedicated to achieving the American dream for all Americans with the golf links, good looks, fair hair, fresh complexions and blue eyes of, say, a Dan Quayle, this winter busied with pursuing a rigorous and well-publicized schedule designed to show him free of any lingering taint of illness or disorder of the sort that would have brought an Erewhonian up for trial "before a jury of his countrymen." If convicted, he was "held up to public scorn and sentenced more or less severely as the case may be." So draconian were the laws of Erewhon—consisting "in the sternest repression of all diseases whatsoever," with "subdivisions of illnesses into crimes and misdemeanors"—that by way of an extreme illustration we are given at detailed length the sentencing of a young man found guilty of "the great crime of laboring under pulmonary consumption" to "imprisonment, with hard labor," to the end of his "miserable existence."

Indeed, the premium placed on health and personal attractiveness, which had led, in the early days of Erewhon, to the public sacrifice of ugly—and, he implies, dark-skinned—interlopers from outlying tribes, persisted in the practice of excluding anyone "too ugly to be allowed to go at large, but not so much so as to be criminally liable," much as their counterparts intruding on us today shun public view under viaducts and in railway tunnels, their numbers expected to decline significantly with the strict enforcement of laws against illegal immigrants promised by the new majority. Coupled with its not unrelated pledge to supplant existing crime-prevention programs with stronger emphasis on prison funding and effective death-penalty provisions, we hear echoes of Erewhon's sentencing judge intoning "if you had been born of healthy and well-to-do parents, and been well taken care of when you were a child, you would never have offended against the laws of your country, nor found yourself in your present disgraceful position."

"Nothing struck me more during my whole sojourn in the country," Butler's narrator observes, "than the general respect for law and order."

As might have been expected, a major deterrent to "renewing American civilization" has been smoked out by the new House Speaker in his blunt notice that it is "impossible to maintain civilization with 12-year-olds having babies," conjuring up once again Butler's kingdom, where the birth of a child was looked on as a painful event, and the pregnancy concealed as long as possible "in anticipation of a severe scolding as soon as the misdemeanor is discovered." For Erewhon was under constant siege by the World of the Unborn clamoring to enter its ranks, drawing lots for prospective parents, each unborn then setting himself to "plague and pester two unfortunate people who had never wronged him, and who were quite contented and happy until he conceived this base design against their peace." Clearly, our own twelve-year-olds are the more vulnerable to the blandishments of the hordes of unborn crowding slums in which religion and sex are the only free diversions available, and love more freely given than parental discipline. And where the Erewhonian baby was kept out of sight until it was able to walk and talk, the architects of this renewal of American civilization, facing the scourge of teenage pregnancies and more than ten million children already living in poverty, propose cutting all aid to mothers under twenty-one and consigning their intrusive offspring to the storied mercies of orphanages and private charities; cutting off aid to all welfare mothers and other recipients after two years whether health care and jobs are there for them or not; and, for good measure, ending Federal support for food stamps and nutrition programs for countless women and noncitizens. As bluntly expressed by the Speaker, "The welfare state kills more poor people in a year than private business."

Embracing the principles of wealth as the measure of power, the millionaire as of greater benefit to society than the beggar and cunning as the guiding policy for all—the projected capital gains tax cuts and indexing, more generous business depreciation and estate and gift tax exclusions, revised laws on liability for defective products and similar arcane provisions in the Contract With America exalt Erewhon's view of money as "the symbol of duty ... the sacrament of having done for mankind that which mankind wanted," holding so high the businessman who has made a fortune "worth 10 professional philanthropists" that the Erewhonian making over £20,000 a year was exempted "from all taxation," considered "as a work of art, and too precious to be meddled with."

"I write with great diffidence, but it seems to me that there is no unfairness in punishing people for their misfortunes, or rewarding them for their sheer good luck." Butler's narrator takes up. "Wherefore should a man be so richly rewarded for having been son to a millionaire, were it not clearly provable that the common welfare is thus better furthered?" We can't help thinking of the recently elected Governor of Texas when reading Butler: "We cannot seriously detract from a man's merit in having been the son of a rich father without imperiling our own tenure of things which we do not wish to jeopardize," since "property *is* robbery, but then, we are all robbers or would-be robbers together, and have found it essential to organize our thieving."

Accordingly, in that land where ill luck "of any kind, or even ill treatment at the hands of others, is considered an offense against society," such breaches of decorum as swindling, check forging, and even outright robbery were treated in hospitals at the public expense; or, if someone in good circumstances perpetrated them, he simply let it be known "to all his friends that he is suffering from a severe fit of immorality . . . and they come and visit him with great solicitude"—much, we may imagine, as the friends of our current Secretary of Commerce, or of the former Democratic head of the House Ways and Means Committee, are currently engaged or, in the spirit of bipartisanship, those of the former President's son Neil Bush, of Silverado fame, and even so blatant a case of deception and mendacity as our gap-toothed Marine colonel lately rehabilitated as a Republican candidate for the United States Senate from Virginia. Such egregious cases were subjected in Erewhon to correction at the hands of "straighteners."

These highly trained specialists had passed their best years at the well-regarded Colleges of Unreason in the diligent study of "hypothetics" and the esoteric "hypothetical language" in which they were "always able to tell a man what is the matter with him as soon as they have heard his story, and their familiarity with the long names assures him that they thoroughly understand his case," thus laying the foundations for the treatment of the many among us today who incline to conceal their ill health, but "are quite open about the most flagrant mental diseases" in the ramshackle mansion later erected in our midst by the father of psychoanalysis himself. Lesser "fits of immorality"—such as the book deals and Gopac funds entangled in the college courses taught by the House Speaker—may be expected to go into remission with the abolition of the House Ethics Committee under his party's proposal to transfer its moribund activities to the House committee charged with handling office space and parking privileges.

"It is not our business to help students to think for themselves," proclaimed the Professor of worldly wisdom at the Colleges of Unreason. "Our duty is to insure that they shall think as we do," largely helping to explain the worship prevalent in Erewhon of the goddess of respectability, Yogrun, whose law was "conformity until absolutely intolerable"—though she was seldom alluded to or even paid the hypocrisy of the kind of lip service that more fully corresponds to the new agenda's call for a constitutional amendment to reintroduce prayer in our public schools and, with a provision strengthening parents' rights in their children's education, opening the classroom to the masked marvel of "creation science."

"To the extent that we stay in the broad area of consensus, we avoid controversy," John Ashcroft, a Republican senator from Missouri, states in a striking tautology worthy of the highest Yogrunite, speaking now to his party's efforts to terminate Federal support for the arts and humanities. In finding unacceptable the use of money wrested from our nation's taxpayers (at some 66 cents a year) to "subsidize an assault on their values, religion or politics" he follows a former czar of education, William J. Bennett, who now casts its agencies as intellectually and morally corrupt in their support of artists and scholars who have undermined our "mainstream American values" as reflected in the art-school curriculum at Erewhon's university, where those studying painting were "examined at frequent intervals in the prices which all the leading pictures of the last 50 or a hundred years" had brought, with their values fluctuating upon being sold and resold. "The artist . . . is a dealer in pictures, and it is as important to him to learn how to adapt his wares to the market, and to know approximately what kind of a picture will fetch how much, as it is for him to be able to paint the picture."

"When we get into the area of challenging some of the fundamental values of American culture, we get ourselves in real trouble," our Missouri senator takes up. He especially rejects any definition of art that means "it has to challenge and be offensive." And given such arguments as these, who can disagree?

Erewhon was originally published at the author's expense, like the rest of his books, excepting, of course, his posthumous work, including the novel *The Way of All Flesh*. He wrote, as one erstwhile editor remarked, "to please himself, and to have something to read in his old age." Of his books Butler himself said, "I never make them; they grow; they come to me and insist upon being written." And it is the "practical side of literature and not the poetical and imaginative—I mean literature applied to the solving of some difficult problem which may be usefully solved—that alone fires me with hot desire to devour and imitate it. That, and the battering down of falsehood to the utmost of my poor ability."

OLD FOES WITH NEW FACES

PRESENTED AT A SYMPOSIUM "The Writer and Religion," organized by William Gass for the International Writers Center at Washington University in St. Louis, October 1994. The essay appeared a year later in *The Yale Review* and was reprinted with the other symposium essays and audience commentary in a collection from the Southern Illinois University Press (2000).

OLD FOES WITH NEW FACES

I have taken my text from a turn on the subtitle of Charles Kingsley's nineteenth-century novel *Hypatia, or New Foes with an Old Face*, the tale of a liberated woman of great beauty, eloquence, modesty, and such brilliance that she came to lead the Christian school of Neoplatonism in fourth-century Alexandria. Her leanings, however, were toward the intellectual rather than the mystical side of Neoplatonic thought, and we are told that when she pushed things too far by taking the pagan prefect of the city for her lover she was torn from her chariot and dragged to the Caesareum, lately become a Christian church, where she was stripped naked, done to death with oyster shells, and burnt by a fanatical Christian mob. Her writings have not survived.

And so the task before us is scarcely a new one. We may think of it as nearer, in the words of T. S. Eliot, to the "fight to recover what has been lost / And found and lost again and again: and now, under conditions / That seem unpropitious." We are asked to explore the relationship between the writer and "one of the earliest and most universal activities of the human mind," as Carl Jung has labeled it, "the eternal problem of religion."

Considering the enormity of this enterprise, I will narrow the focus of my remarks at the outset to my own pursuits. By writers, I assume we mean writers of fiction; by religion, the one I have barked my shins against for over half a century in one or another of its avatars, to borrow an epithet (as Christianity itself has never hesitated to do when it has served its purposes). Rather than initiating our undertaking with a confrontation—I am sure we will see plenty of that—I propose to extend the hand of fellowship from the criterion central to both: that which constitutes poetic faith for the writer in Coleridge's familiar "willing suspension of disbelief," and for the religionist the leap of faith enshrined in Augustine's misquotation of Tertullian, "Credo quia absurdum."

In other words, we are all in the same line of business: that of concocting, arranging, and peddling fictions to get us safely through the night.

Religion, as defined by Jung, is the term that "designates the attitude peculiar to a consciousness which has been altered by the experience of the numinosum"—the supernatural, that which is mysterious, spiritually inhabited, impossible to describe or to understand. In more mundane terms it might be seen as analogous to a legal fiction, in which the court, obliged to support its decision in resolving a controversy, makes and adopts a factual assumption which is not based on reality, thus driving us inevitably into the teeth of Voltaire's stale aphorism "If God did not exist, it would be necessary to invent him."

It takes little effort of the imagination to picture primitive man, assailed by plague and accident, floods, thunder, lightning, and, perhaps most potently—as Sir James Frazer would have it—by fear of the human dead. Eventually he abandons the charms, spells, and sorcery devised to hold such calamities at bay and seeks refuge in rituals of prayer and supplication, as magic despairs and becomes religion. "It would be a regrettable mistake," writes Jung, "if anybody should understand my observations to be a kind of proof of the existence of God. They prove only the existence of an archetypal image of the Deity." Among the most prominent of these was the one to emerge from Aristotle's Unmoved Mover in Thomas Aquinas's application of reason (as opposed to revelation, with its taint of the mystical), arguing for a God as the First and Uncaused Cause, flowering in the concept of theism positing a Creator immanent and everywhere present, and so open to every interpretation from the sublime to the ridiculous. Among the latter, for example, a recent sampling turns up the assertion by sometime critic and failed novelist George Steiner that "any coherent account of the capacity of human speech to communicate meaning and feeling is, in the final analysis, underwritten by the assumption of God's presence."

Hearkening to "the present testimony of the sense" untinged by paranoia, it had long since fallen far more coherently to the Scottish philosopher David Hume to pull the rug from under not only a God as the First and Uncaused Cause, but the entire order of Efficient Causes, denying the entrenched idea of any necessary connection between phenomena, which he ascribed to "habit breeding expectation," thereby reducing the "principle of causation" to nothing more than the mind's propensity to make believe, to pretend, fabricate, invent—in other words, to concoct a convenient fiction.

Certainly an enhanced capacity for self-delusion is a valuable attribute for the writer in nurturing both his fictional characters and, often enough, his own. Thus it is hardly surprising to find this capacity to be fueled by an equally large appetite for strong drink: the majority of America's native-born winners of the Nobel Prize in literature have been confirmed alcoholics. We may even go so far as to find their counterpart in Alfred North Whitehead's remark that "a relic of the religious awe at intoxication is the use of wine in the Communion service"—at all odds a relic of the drunken license turned loose at pagan saturnalias of a still earlier time where, habit breeding expectation, promiscuous intercourse provided plentiful material for the marvels of virgin birth that followed. "Speaking for instance of the motive of the virgin birth," Jung cautions us again that he is "only concerned with the fact that there is such an idea" but not "whether such an idea is true or false in any other sense."

The priest is the guardian of mysteries, the artist is driven to expose them. The manifest difference between them is that the writer is a teller of secrets who grapples with his audience one reader, one page at a time; where the priest engages the collective delusion of his entire congregation all at once. Accordingly, our ubiquitous polls count nine in ten of our countrymen saying they have never doubted God's existence, eight in ten expecting to be called before him on judgment day, seven in ten planning on life after death, and more than half believing in angels. Outnumbering supporters of reincarnation by three to one, almost three-quarters opt for a heaven where good lives on earth will be eternally rewarded, with more than half basking in the company of God and Jesus, but fewer than half within that of friends, relatives, and spouses. Oddly enough under these circumstances, only 5 percent expect eternity to be boring.

Hopelessly earthbound, an implacable malcontent named E. M. Cioran tears a leaf from the deists, who oppose theism's (and George Steiner's) immanent, omnipresent God with one who has simply set his handiwork in motion and walked away: "Contemplating this botched Creation," he asks, "how can we help incriminating its Author, how—above all—suppose him able and adroit? Any other God would have given evidence of more competence or more equilibrium than this one: errors and confusion wherever you look!" We have here, in effect, a recipe for the steaming dish being served up at the literary banquets of postmodernism, structuralism, and deconstruction under the name *aporia*. Its ingredients—"difference, discontinuity, disparity, contradiction, discord, ambiguity, irony, paradox, perversity, opacity, obscurity, anarchy, chaos"—are thus catalogued by the conservative historian Gertrude Himmelfarb, and then excoriated, along with postmodernism's chief cooks and bottle washers who celebrate this stew of relativism over the search for "truth." Jesting Pilate can scarcely be blamed for leaving without an answer.

This relativism, which seems to have taken on the pejorative mantle of secularism in the lexicon of the true believers, is "concrete, pluralistic, inductive, historical, skeptical and intimately bound up with deference to experience," in the words of the liberal historian Arthur Schlesinger Jr. Absolutism, on the other hand, is "abstract, monistic, deductive, ahistorical, solemn, and it is intimately bound up with deference to authority."

In the religious arena, the distinction is aptly carried over by Jung in examining the Catholic role, "where the Protestant point of view of an individual relationship to God is overpowered by mass organization and correspondingly collective religious feeling." Thus the Catholic "who has turned his back on the church usually develops a secret or manifest inclination toward atheism, whereas the Protestant follows, if possible, a sectarian movement. The absolutism of the Catholic church seems to demand an equally absolute negation, while Protestant relativism permits variations."

"The argument is not whether Catholics should leave their tradition or whether they stay for the right reasons," counters the popular apologist Reverend Andrew M. Greeley, relishing the fact that Catholicism "is not a democracy." Extolling the church as "resolutely authoritarian," Father Greeley blithely offers us such glaring instances as its discrimination against women and homosexuals, its intrusions on behavior in the marital bedroom, its anti-abortion stance everywhere and proscription of birth control even where famine, disease, and overpopulation reign, its repression of disagreement and dissent, and its having looked quietly the other way for decades in the face of sexual abuses by its priests. "But let the charges stand for the sake of argument," he concludes, handily ducking the entire issue by default, finding refuge in the make-believe monumental mischief perpetrated by David Hume two centuries ago. "How can 85 percent of those who are born Catholic remain, one way or another, in the church?" Greeley asks. "Catholics like their heritage because it has great stories," and there is no shortage of those spawned along the way, some dating back six centuries to the *Decameron*, the work of one of Italy's greatest poets, Giovanni Boccaccio.

"Catholics have sex more often than other Americans," Father Greeley persists, ever divisive, and "are more playful in their erotic amusements than others." The *Decameron* bears him out in many of its tales: a woman is tricked by an imposter priest into believing that he is the angel Gabriel and has fallen in love with her; after solacing himself with her, he escapes in a cloud of feathers, leaving his wings behind; elsewhere, an abbess surprised *in delicto* pulls the errant priest's pants over her head, mistaking them in the dark for her cowl. Then there is the story of the nuns who coax a youth feigning mutism to service the entire convent— till one hot day the abbess finds him stretched out, apparently asleep. But "the wind lifting the forepart of his clothes," she discovers his attraction and seizes upon him for herself.

"Catholics," Father Greeley confides elsewhere, abruptly turning from the church's authoritarianism for Jehovah's, "are more likely than others to picture God as a Mother, a Lover, a Spouse and a Friend (as opposed to a Father, a Judge, a Master and a King)"—parenthetically impaling the Jews on Mark Twain's observation that the Old Testament "gives us the picture of these people's Deity as he was before he got religion, the other one gives us a picture of him as he appeared afterward." Such sentiments had a generous boost from Pope John Paul II himself when he noted Old Testament instances of the Jewish people's "infidelity to God" and recommended "the coming of the Holy Spirit at Pentecost as the fulfillment of the new and everlasting covenant between God and humanity," a covenant "sealed in the blood of Jesus" and foretold by the Prophets, who were sent "to call the people to conversion, to warn them of their hardness of heart and foretell a new covenant still to come." A good century ago, in fact, this "perfect gift from above" had been visited on another benighted community right here at home, where "from the farthest realms of morning came the Black-Robe chief, the Prophet in a birch canoe with paddles, he the Priest of Prayer, the Paleface with his message to the people, told the purport of his mission, told them of the Virgin Mary and her blessed Son, the Saviour, how he lived on earth as we do, how he fasted, prayed and laboured, how the Jews, the tribe accursed, mocked him, scourged him, crucified him" in the American grain of bigotry and the poetic faith of Henry Wadsworth Longfellow.

Not to be outdone in this realm of great stories, Boccaccio gives us Abraham the Jew, who goes to Rome at the instigation of a friend bent on converting him to "enquire into the manners and fashions of the Pope and Cardinals and other prelates." Finding them all from the highest to the lowest "universally gluttons, winebibbers, drunkards and slaves to their bellies," and given over to lust, sodomy, simony, and greed, he returns home so deeply impressed by the ascendancy of the Holy Spirit—it is "true and holy over any other" because it has triumphed over the depredations of the clergy and thereby raises the Christian religion to heights "still brighter and more glorious"—that he demands to be baptized forthwith.

Confronted by such a dazzling array of old foes with new faces, why not stop being a priest and leave the church? "Why should I leave?" our present-day apologist responds, quoting a friend: "Luther tried that and it didn't work!" Didn't work? The man almost single-handedly sparked the Reformation by proclaiming every individual Christian's right to free himself, or even herself, from priestly bondage. This unleashed the Protestant movement throughout the Western world, a movement of such wide appeal that it now appears in the pied garb of some four hundred denominations asserting their liberation from the papal yoke by bickering among themselves at every opportunity.

After dropping by nearly a third following the harsh view of birth control displayed in the papal encyclical of 1968, about a quarter of our population remains Catholic "one way or another," as Father Greeley puts it, apparently accommodating those "cafeteria Catholics" who can't swallow the full menu. But of the 86.5 percent of Americans calling themselves Christians (wherein the largest Protestant denomination counts 15 million Southern Baptists), these frenzied times have taken their greatest toll among the pillars of Protestant society. The Episcopalians, leading the way, have fallen 28 percent, from 3.4 to 2.5 million over twenty-five years; Presbyterians are down by 25 percent, from 4 to 3 million; the United Methodist Church by 18 percent, from 11 to 9.2 million; the United Church of Christ by 20 percent, and the Disciples of Christ by 42 percent. Their coffers are depleted, their great stories threadbare.

Then picture this: at a time of social and religious ferment in the early nineteenth century, a fourteen-year-old farm boy off alone in the woods seeking spiritual guidance is abruptly descended upon by two luminous beings—presumably God and Jesus—and soon followed by a heavenly messenger resurrected for the purpose of unearthing a set of gold plates he had hidden in a nearby hillside some fourteen centuries before. These plates, inscribed in a mysterious tongue with an account of certain American Indians' descent from an ancient Israelite colony, prove to contain the truths of Christ's Gospel when translated with the help of a codebook supplied by this resurrected prophet, Moroni.

About four years later, in 1827, that text emerges as the Book of Mormon; its author, the founder of the eponymous church, will be lynched for his trouble some seventeen years later by a mob in the Middle West. In his extraordinary way, he anticipates the modern "scriptor" dear to the hearts of the deconstructionists, who is "born simultaneously with the text, is in no way equipped with a being preceding or exceeding the writing, is not the subject with the book as predicate" described by Roland Barthes in *The Death of the Author*. "We know now that a text is not a line of words releasing a single 'theological' meaning (the 'message' of the Author-God) but a multi-dimensional space in which a variety of writings, none of them original, blend and clash," which is one way to explain the continuing worldwide success of the Church of Jesus Christ of Latter-day Saints.

Patriarchal, hierarchal, rigorously authoritarian, forbidding gambling, risqué movies, alcohol, tobacco, and even coffee and tea, binding its members by church law to give as much as 10 percent of their incomes (which brings in almost $5 billion a year), and dispatching as missionaries over fifty thousand believers at their own expense, the Mormon Church in this same past twenty-five years has grown from under two to more than eight million members in 120 countries. It is one of the most rapidly growing denominations in the world.

Since nothing can be given which cannot also be withheld, the fruits of the Founder's divine revelation in the jealous grip of the church hierarchs are dispensed in strict accordance with Mormon doctrine, and encroached upon by those below at the peril of disfellowship and excommunication, leaving no room for apostasy and very little indeed for cafeteria Mormons. Quite as "resolutely authoritarian," the Catholic Church, with almost a billion members, is obviously less amenable to such close discipline—despite the good offices of Opus Dei and a pope saddled with great stories cast as dogma by his infallible predecessors, among them the bodily assumption of the Virgin Mary into heaven. This great story has provoked the observation elsewhere that, traveling at a speed consistent with breathing, she would not yet have reached the nearest of the fixed stars. While sharing a belief in a Mother in heaven, both churches forbid women the priesthood, but while that of the Mormons proliferates (it allows boys of twelve to distribute the sacrament, to baptize at sixteen, and to become bishops in their early twenties), the number of Catholic seminarians has declined by one-half despite Father Greeley's assurance that "research indicates that priests are among the happiest men in America." In addition, the rising tide of lay teachers displacing nuns threatens to overwhelm what he calls "that brilliant American Catholic innovation, the parochial school"; and even the Sacrament of Reconciliation, embedding "in ritual and mystery the deeply held Catholic story of second chances," appears menaced by a paucity of priests to man the confessionals where, almost five centuries ago, simony and flagrant corruption drove Martin Luther to burst the authoritarian grip of the papacy on divine revelation sealed in the blood of Jesus and open the barn door for each individual Christian to have a direct relationship to God and experience the descent of the Holy Ghost and perhaps be born again as a Pentecostal-charismatic, an Evangelical, a Moonie, indeed any one of the fifty million Fundamentalists who range across the country today, each—like Stephen Leacock's Lord Ronald, flinging himself upon his horse and riding madly off in all directions—proclaiming the inerrancy of the Bible, laying on hands, speaking in tongues, handling snakes, and converting the

Jews to speed up the Second Coming and the end of the world envisioned in the "multi-dimensional space in which a variety of writings, none of them original, blend and clash" in the supreme, ultimate, hair-raising great story detailed in the Revelation of St. John the Divine Scriptor from his banishment on the barren Aegean island of Patmos in the year 95, enough to drive anyone round the bend. There an angel bursts into his humble grotto to introduce Alpha and Omega with the voice of a trumpet saying, "What thou seest, write in a book," and proceeds to dictate a scenario replete with the sun turning black, the stars falling, and the sea turning to blood, as well as fire, earthquake, and the four horsemen, all of them delivering torment and punishment of such apocalyptic dimensions as sorely to try the willing suspension of disbelief wherever reason reigns.

But reason, as Mae West said of goodness when complimented on her beautiful diamonds, has nothing to do with it. Nor need it: for the King James version along with Shakespeare's works are the most glorious achievements in English literature, and the sheer splendor of the English Bible and the images and prophecies of its last book are so formidable that those millions suffused with Jung's numinosum who seek refuge from the clamorous celebration of aporia castigated by Gertrude Himmelfarb embrace its inerrancy against all comers. Their truth is not, perhaps, the pristine, solemn, monistic Truth pursued by Himmelfarb, but it is similarly authoritarian and absolute for all that, subscribing to the same fundamental tenets, differing in little but degree and emphasis, and unleashed broadcast by those twin Pandora's boxes that shape and reshape our world daily, radio, and television.

Among the most rapidly growing of these Christian sects, the Pentecostal-charismatics are directly moved, in life and prayer, by the Holy Spirit and born again through taking Jesus as their personal savior. To this doctrine the Evangelicals, "on fire with God" (and games and rock bands), add the need to press for conversion of the Jews, whose only role, in their covenant with God, is seen as preparing for the new covenant making Christians the chosen people. And putting the literal truth of the Bible first, the Fundamentalists generally look forward to the end time for human history in the final battle between good and evil at Armageddon. They revel in the words of the Divine Scriptor, "And I heard a voice from heaven saying unto me, Write, blessed are the dead which die in the Lord from henceforth," and all that unbridled revelation impatiently anticipates the Lord in 1 Thessalonians descending from heaven with a shout when "the dead in Christ shall rise first" and the born-again survivors are "caught up together with them in the clouds, to meet the Lord in the air" and be with him forever.

"How then can it be," asks Mark Twain's Fallen Angel in his second Letter from the Earth, "that the human being, like the immortals, naturally places sexual intercourse far and away above all other joys—yet he has left it out of his heaven! The very thought of it excites him; opportunity sets him wild; in this state he will risk life, reputation, everything," as our occasional hellfire Christian broadcasters, contesting Father Greeley's frolicsome Catholics, seem literally hell-bent on proving. Eve the Temptress prevails in that most lurid invention in all of Christian theology: the story with a leaf from Augustine wherein Adam, banished from Paradise with "his spouse—who was the cause of his sin and the companion of his damnation—would drag through the ages the burden of Original Sin," leaving humanity "wallowing in evil"; while women, whose only function was childbearing, as

Karen Armstrong observes in her excellent book *A History of God*, "passed the contagion of Original Sin to the next generation, like a venereal disease." This posed a dilemma of sorts for the God who'd exhorted the happy couple he'd created to "be fruitful, and multiply, and replenish the earth"; a good thousand pages later, he finished off both his Creation and his Revelation to our exhausted Scriptor with "Write: for these words are true and faithful. And he said unto me, It is done," having cast the nonbelievers, liars, murderers, and whoremongers into the lake of fire and brimstone.

"Life was not a valuable gift," in Mark Twain's view, but "death was man's best friend; when man could endure life no longer, death came and set him free. In time, the Deity perceived that death was a mistake," for "while it was an admirable agent for the inflicting of misery upon the survivor, it allowed the dead person to escape from all further persecution in the blessed refuge of the grave. This was not satisfactory. A way must be contrived to pursue the dead beyond the tomb. The Deity pondered this matter during four thousand years unsuccessfully, but as soon as he came down to earth and became a Christian his mind cleared and he knew what to do. He invented hell, and proclaimed it."

Its chief tenant, to be turned loose after a thousand years' sojourn in the bottomless pit for just long enough to cause wholesale mischief here on earth until another rain of fire from heaven sends him back to be tormented day and night forever and ever, is apparently still at large in America. A Gallup poll has recently counted more than half the Baptists believing in a personal devil; among Catholics, he is repudiated by one in five but held to be an impersonal evil force by twice that number, and a personal being by about one-third. With "habit breeding expectation," in Hume's phrase, he reportedly makes himself known with four signs of diabolical possession: levitation, abnormal strength, knowledge of things his victims have never heard of, and languages they've never studied. One Catholic priest in the Archdiocese of New York was inspired to permit the filming for television of a real-life exorcism performed on a troubled sixteen-year-old girl as a way to encourage belief in the devil's existence and give accurate information on the church's measures for relief. His bishop approved, citing what he "believed to be the good of the church," and noting that "the devil really exists" and "is powerful and actively at work in the world"; the cardinal sermonized that demonic possession calling for exorcism seemed very rare; while the pope was reported to have expanded the number of priests performing exorcisms in the land where Boccaccio had, centuries since, given the ritual a new twist in his tale of a young monk named Rustico, whose hermit life is abruptly interrupted by an unblemished maiden seeking to learn how she may best serve God. Assured that God's greatest enemy is the devil, who should be put back into hell at every opportunity, she follows his instructions for doing so: she kneels beside him, naked as he is, and marvels at the unfamiliar resurrection of the flesh thrusting forth and readily identified by her host as the devil incarnate. Then, learning that she herself is hell's custodian, the maiden pleases God and Rustico so diligently that the devil is returned there six times before the conceit is taken from his head and he abides at peace—a ritual so often repeated that the poor monk is consumed, and she returns to the city to marry a young gallant who readily lends himself to the Lord's service in the manner prescribed.

Down the centuries innumerable men of God have followed the recipe of the young monk Rustico for laying the devil to rest in fact and fiction. Most recently, two broadcast evangelists from the Assemblies of God made headlines with adultery and fornication and got off a good deal easier than Onan, who, in Mark Twain's account, "was commanded to 'go in unto his brother's wife'—which he did, but instead of finishing, 'he spilled it on the ground.' The Lord slew Onan for that, for the Lord never could abide indelicacy." Given the stakes these days, onanism, however indelicate, takes its place alongside free condom distribution to fiery teenagers in the explosive issue of birth control. At its most painfully divisive extreme, where abortion is concerned, offenders are punished, as Onan was, with death. Thus the director of the Christian action group to which the shotgun slayer of the doctor entering a Florida abortion clinic belonged was moved to observe, "He simply carried out his theology."

"Given the stakes—life itself—we can do no less," echoes New York's archbishop, commenting on the decision of the nation's Roman Catholic bishops to spend $3 to $5 million on a national campaign opposing abortion, which involved a public relations giant whose other clients include makers of oral contraceptives, condoms, and intrauterine devices, as well as Playboy Enterprises. It makes obvious sense for the Catholic Church to oppose birth control, which would simply result in fewer Catholics, as does the warning from the most egregious of the so-called pro-life Christian broadcasters that it would reduce the number of future taxpayers. Naturally, both groups oppose homosexuality, which swells the number of neither. The Old Testament's condemnation of homoerotic escapades, brought to the fore recently in the hubbub over whether St. Paul was gay or merely epileptic, continues to blossom: the priestly dilemma of pederasty is now seen in the unwelcome, sobering light of church liability. A few years ago, Catholic diocesan insurers paid $4.2 million to a half-dozen families, which still left another dozen suits pending with another $100 million in the balance.

"Orthodoxy is my doxy—heterodoxy is another man's doxy," as an eighteenth-century bishop of Gloucester explained, using the current slang for a loose woman to do so, and the two embrace again in the dismay of an Orthodox Israeli rabbi over his country's invasion by dinosaurs pictured everywhere from movies to cereal boxes as "millions of years old, despite the fact that the world was created only 5,753 years ago," and the fundamentalist masquerade that parades Genesis as "Creation Science" in renegade American schoolrooms today. Conflicting fossil evidence is blithely banished with the handy fiction that any God capable of creating the world would certainly have been able to produce a history to go with it, taking us back a full century to the monumental collision between long-established Christian beliefs and the shattering advent of Darwinism.

Did Jesus really write the Lord's Prayer? Did he fake the Resurrection, as further current speculation has it, by playing dead till he was taken down and spirited away by friends in order to create what Father Greeley exalts as "the most graceful story of all"? Is the wall between church and state erected in the Establishment Clause breached in lowering New Hampshire's state flag to half-mast on Good Friday to honor Jesus as a historical personage? Or was this historical Jesus himself a fiction, and, finally, would it make any difference in the transcendental view of all mortal creation as the fiction promulgated by Bishop Berkeley which Doctor Johnson refuted with a kick at a large stone. This, at any rate, was the route taken by Mary Baker Eddy in her "discovery" of Christian Science.

In the late nineteenth century's gallery of pseudoscience, a collection teeming with animal magnetism, mesmerism, phrenology, and theosophy, Kant's earlier efforts to refute Hume's "present testimony of the senses" with a fiercely reasoned metaphysics rose supreme, and the ball was passed, as from Tinker to Evers to Chance, from Kant to Hegel to Mrs. Eddy. The only thorn in Mrs. Eddy's side, however, was that her "discovery" of the religion she founded took place neither in the putative throes of divine revelation nor even through the Hegelian derivation of Kant but, considering Mrs. Eddy's severely limited intellectual resources, via a monograph by an accredited scholar named Francis Lieber which provided the plagiarized text forming the body of her gospel, *Science and Health with Key to the Scriptures.*

Here, Lieber's "Hegel's science brings to light Truth and its supremacy, universal harmony, God's entirety, and matter's nothingness" becomes "Christian Science brings to light Truth and its supremacy, universal harmony, the entireness of God, good, and the nothingness of evil." Again, "Properly, there is no physical science. The Principle of science is God, intelligence and not matter" becomes "There is no physical science, inasmuch as all truth proceeds from the divine Mind" and "The Principle of divine metaphysics is God." And again, "That Spirit propagates matter or matter spirit, is morally impossible. Hegel repudiates the thought" becomes simply "If matter is first, it cannot produce Mind. Like produces like." "The science of Being reverses every belief of the senses. Socrates understood this when pledging the superiority of Spirit over matter in a cup of hemlock poison" appears as "Science reverses the evidence of material sense. . . . Because he understood the superiority and immortality of good, Socrates feared not the hemlock poison." And so on, again, and again, and again. "Mrs. Eddy did not concentrate her plagiarisms,"

Lieber's commentator observes, "she scattered them like the leaves of autumn," as elsewhere "for Kant and Hegel, it would not be a serious drawback to Christianity if Jesus proved to be a pure fiction" is paired with "In similar vein Mrs. Eddy affirms it would make no difference to her if Jesus had never existed" since the spiritual Christos prevails in both, rendering the historic Jesus inconsequential.

In the pulsing American vein, however, what has never appeared inconsequential to the Church of Christ, Scientist is its patriotic belief in money. When a $100 million bequest was promised the church under the wills of two California sisters on condition that it publish a book in their hands that portrayed Mrs. Eddy as a divine figure who fulfilled biblical prophecy and offer it in the 2,500 Christian Science reading rooms throughout the country, else the money would go to two other candidates, the church balked but finally gave in with an ambiguously worded imprimatur. Later, an agreement filed in court left it with 53 percent of the ransom; the rest was to be divided between the protesting candidates, Stanford University and the Los Angeles County Museum of Art. Striking more deadly to the heart of the matter, the death of an eleven-year-old boy with diabetes who'd been treated with Mrs. Eddy's formulas, which hold all physical ailments to be brought about by "error," alienation from God, and other spiritual infections, cost Mother Church another $9 million in the first wrongful-death lawsuit to be brought against it in this clouded contest between Mind and matter.

In turbulent times like today's, established denominations already prey to dissension within their own ranks are shouldered aside by sects which threaten to degenerate into cults in all-engulfing collisions with reality which fill the courts: clergy malpractice suits in cases of suicide, American Indian use of peyote during sacred rituals, Santeria's animal sacrifice. Some merely provide an innocent confusion of realms, like the four-foot-high phallus-shaped stone parking barrier in Golden Gate Park that was briefly worshipped by local Hindus as a shrine to Shiva, god of destruction, or the yoga class shut down by Baptist, Lutheran, and Church of God protesters in Georgia who saw it as a branch of Eastern mysticism that would open the door to the devil; and others ending in Jonestown, in Waco, in two small Swiss villages, in the Tokyo subways.

"Religion is the last refuge of human savagery," Whitehead writes. "Indeed history, down to the present day, is a melancholy record of the horrors which can attend religion: human sacrifice, and in particular the slaughter of children, cannibalism, sensual orgies, abject superstition, hatred as between races, the maintainance of degrading customs, hysteria, bigotry, all can be laid at its charge."

Once upon a time, fiction was a way of getting at some kind of truth: we concocted fictions to get us through the night or, nostalgic for absolutes, we embraced revelation as ultimate Truth. Now fiction is used to bring on the darkest night of all, in which historical reality in its most monstrous epiphany is dismissed as a mischievous, fictive concoction by the so-called Holocaust revisionists, a deceptively mild label for those bent on giving subance to Hitler's maxim that any lie will pass muster provided it is big enough. This denial, made in the face of all the tangible evidence and all the witnesses, living and dead, of the systematic murder of six million human beings of different race and religion, is a lie of such enormous proportions that it will live on and reemerge to taint history forever. It offers the worst-case scenario of the willing suspension of disbelief.

In short, "Who do you believe?" Groucho Marx asked. "Me? or your own eyes?"

OCCASIONAL WRITINGS

THE FIRST TWO PIECES COLLECTED HERE, although they were never published, were worked over several times by Gaddis and submitted under the pressure of current events, including the Savings and Loan scandal under the first Bush Administration and budgetary aggression coming out of Newt Gingrich's 104th Congress that would decimate the National Endowment for the Arts. In his cover letter to Howard Goldberg of the Op-Ed page of *The New York Times*, Gaddis (in response evidently to another editor's suggested cuts) defends the "tight coherency" of the S&L piece and especially the opening citational "flow"—from the religious fanaticism of Gerald Mayo to Reagan's get-rich credo to Keynes on a future universal wealth. Gaddis protests that it all "follows so closely right to the end that it would be very painful to cut further"—although he also says he "would yield the opening sentence if so pressed."

That sentence has been retained here: it is of course a version of the "old saw" that Gaddis would use again, four years later, to open *A Frolic of His Own*: "Justice?—You get justice in the next world, in this world you have the law."

The squib on Dan Quayle was written in response to a survey conducted by the editors of *Esquire* magazine.

THIS ABOVE ALL

"We will find justice in the next world; in this world we have the law." Take the case of one Gerald Mayo who, back in the Nixon years, sought to file a civil rights suit *in forma pauperis* against Satan who, he alleged, had "on numerous occasions caused plaintiff misery and unwarranted threats" placing "deliberate obstacles in his path" bringing on his ruinous downfall.

Had not another true believer urged his fellow Christians not to "let Satan win the day," posing material wealth as "God's way of blessing people who put Him first"? And today, with two-thirds of the country's abundance in the hands of a tenth of the population, 1,500,000 millionaires bask under the Rev. Jerry Falwell's imprimatur while half the populace huddles over 4 percent of the national wealth, and one in four is born into poverty where, by Senator Daniel Moynihan's count, we have become "the first nation in history in which the poorest group in the population" is the children, and the poorest of those the youngest.

Thus while the Mayo complaint contained no allegation of the defendant maintaining residence in his jurisdiction, Federal Judge Weber in dismissing the plea confronted the problem whether the suit, if allowed to proceed, could be maintained as a class action "where the class is so numerous that joinder of all members is impracticable" *UNITED STATES ex rel. Gerald Mayo v. SATAN AND HIS STAFF* (Misc. No. 5357, U.S. District Court W.D. Pennsylvania, 1971), noting specifically that the complaint failed to supply an address where the U.S. Marshall could serve papers and so, in effect, consigning plaintiff and defendant together to that swelling throng "who are sleeping on grates," in President Reagan's later felicitous embrace, "the homeless, who are homeless, you might say, by choice."

Here, seen through a glass darkly (you might say), shone the allegiance displayed elsewhere in his simplistic credo "What I want to see above all is that this remains a country where some-one can always get rich."

Conjecturing on "the economic possibilities for our grandchil-dren" just sixty years ago, Lord Keynes remarked that the day might not be all that far off when everybody would be rich. We shall then, the late British economist E. F. Schumacher quotes him, "once more value ends above means, and prefer the useful. But beware! The time for all this is not yet. For at least another hundred years we must pretend to ourselves and to everyone that fair is foul and foul is fair; for foul is useful and fair is not. Avarice and usury and precaution must be our gods for a little longer still. For only they can lead us out of the tunnel of economic necessity into daylight." That light at the end of the tunnel, we have now learned, was the train roaring toward us throughout the Reagan-Bush decade, its hour come round at last in the crash of the Sav-ings and Loan industry bearing its explosive $500 billion cargo greater than the cost of all of World War II down upon those very grandchildren over the next generation.

The massive theft and corruption of the late nineteenth cen-tury's Gilded Age, to which the current S&L debacle has been compared, did after all produce the railroads, manufactories, whole industries that led us to become the world's greatest creditor, while today—still thirsting for a fraud we can believe in—the party politicians seek some way to cling to that old "Reagan magic" which transformed us to the world's greatest debtor, sweeping before it public and private debt from $4.2 to some

$10 trillion, turning Keynesian theory on its head with a flourishing $169 billion current Federal deficit devouring one-quarter of our income tax receipts simply to pay the interest on the borrowed money. No wonder that the most egregious of our Christian broadcasters and sometime presidential aspirant was prompted to bemoan the outcome of legalized abortion for depriving us of future taxpayers, and others of us to recall Anatole France's preference for the rogue over the fool since the rogue does at least take a rest sometimes, the fool never.

Our Attorney General prefers the rogue, who with a name like Fail at least provides headlines, forecasting a mere five years of "sustained effort" to prosecute the "most serious" hundred cases of S&L fraud which President Bush himself belatedly promises to back up with "teams of razor-sharp prosecutors and auditors." The hundreds of S&L properties already confiscated by the government now found to be teeming with toxic wastes assure him an ever widening multibillion arena for redeeming his pledge to be our "environmental president," just as his posture as our "education president" faces vastly expanded opportunities with the collapse of the Student Loan program where those most in need of its benefits, if they rather than the taxpayers were ever to repay their indebtedness, will obviously be among the first to swell the ranks of those sixty million functional and marginal illiterates out there crowding the fringes of our society today.

In the more exclusionary realm of higher education, "I thought it would be a good learning experience" was the way the President's "most sensitive" (or second most) son described his matriculation at Silverado: no student loans here, unless one so regards the "attractive mortgage terms" on his $300 thousand home, the $100 thousand loan on the side for a soured investment which he then declared a gift, or the highly imaginative financing surrounding his original $100 investment in the JNB oil enterprise with its subsequent $900 thousand line of credit, altogether leaving the taxpayers with a tuition bill of roughly $1 billion upon Silverado's default which he has labeled "inconsequential." Still, half his countrymen feel that his close scrutiny by Federal investigators is unfair, supporting Schumacher interpreting "foul is useful and fair is not," "Ethical considerations are not merely irrelevant, they are an actual hindrance . . ."

Even the heretofore supine Congressional Democrats have been aroused to propose a "savings and loan enforcement package" and to boot, a commission to examine the roots of the crisis which were, if they'd dared to look, laid bare scarcely a score of years ago when Schumacher went straight to the heart of the matter. "If human vices such as greed and envy are systematically cultivated," he wrote then, "the inevitable result is nothing less than a collapse of intelligence. A man driven by greed or envy loses the power of seeing things as they really are, of seeing things in their roundness and wholeness, and his very successes become failures. If whole societies become infected by these vices, they may achieve astonishing things but they become increasingly incapable of solving the most elementary problems of everyday existence."

And so we lift despairing eyes from the front-page picture of our four living Republican ex-presidents at the dedication of that $21 million museum of detritus masquerading as a "library" at Yorba Linda, California, through the clouds of white doves and fifty thousand red, white, and blue balloons mingling with the ascending prayers of Reverends Billy Graham and Norman Vincent Peale, to the greater heights of Mount Rushmore searching (above all and in vain), for some (you might say) moral equivalent of our Founding Fathers.

J. DANFORTH QUAYLE

J. Danforth Quayle, that dangling initial tells the story: the pompous self-importance of your small-town banker who forecloses the farm, your Gulf War general with the $5 million advance whose selective chronicle of slaughter is being written by someone else; J. Danforth Quayle, the acolyte of the reigning prince of hypocrites (two patrician middle initials this time): J. Danforth Quayle, who has in fact got principles of his own, derived from an abiding confusion of an elitism based on merit with a midwestern country-club version embracing the empty privileges of unearned money; and who is not the public joke so frequently portrayed but rather, in being smart rather than intelligent, using the vested interests that are using him, could, if allowed by a skipped heartbeat or a dazed electorate, emerge as quite a dangerous fellow.

ON CREATIVE WRITING
AND THE NATIONAL ENDOWMENT
FOR THE ARTS

Earlier this year I agreed to serve on a panel of the Literature Program for Creative Writing Fellowships under the grant procedure of the National Endowment for the Arts "dedicated to foster excellence, diversity and vitality of the Arts in the United States."

Each twelve-member panel was divided into four groups (a similar approach prevailed in the separate realm of poetry), each panelist assigned the reading of 325 manuscripts of up to thirty pages each of some 1,100 submissions. Aside from the modest honorarium, the summer devoured by these readings seemed sometimes to become a season of penance for the NEA grant I received years ago to complete my own second novel after a twenty-year hiatus. There was no scamping our assignment: each manuscript, identified only by an anonymous number, bore an orange card upon which to enter critical comments and evaluation, like grading a vast and faceless creative writing class of every stripe and level of competence.

Still, from this morass of stories and chapters from works in progress ranging from overblown anecdotes to colourful travelogues and childhood reminiscences, from slick professional efforts derived from television and bad reading to bleak real life confessionals, there would suddenly emerge something hugely original, witty, agonizing or simply touching, elegantly perceived and executed: the wrenching desolation of the nineteenth-century frontier and of today's small town America, of reservation Indians, struggling Hispanics and black voices coming off the page to tear your heart open, sexual confusion and homoerotic torments, nuns in Alaska, Jews in Mexico and Hawaiians in California, the pregnant girl disowned, the suicidal mother, the tragicomic aspirations of a Puerto Rican beauty contest. From all these each panelist was to recommend twelve for grant fellowships totaling 144, to be further winnowed down in a second round and the final three-day conference.

Since 1990, nineteen of the twenty-four winners of the National Book Award, the National Book Critics Circle and Pulitzer prizes had received NEA fellowships. Last year, with reduced funding levels, 3 percent of all applications were funded, and of this current lot, 2 percent; the granting side of the Endowment's seventeen programs for all the arts has been trimmed to four, the staff cut by 40 percent this year, by a further 40 percent scheduled for next year, and, to complete the massacre, by 20 percent the year following, leaving us high and dry among civilized nations to embrace the death penalty both literally and figuratively.

Traditionally, we have cherished the arts as entertainment and decoration, complementing our decorous myth of life, liberty and the pursuit of happiness. "I like beautiful things," mouths Senator Jesse Helms (ever get a look at Mrs. Helms?), echoing a Norman Rockwell America where Henry Clay Frick sits enthroned under a Raphael reading the *Saturday Evening Post*, while House Speaker Newt Gingrich's Republican majority concentrates on returning us to the Golden Age of those Robber Barons against a backdrop featuring 1 percent of the nation's households holding 40 percent of its wealth, as both Congressional leaders lead the hue and cry against any and all of the arts being subsidized by taxpayer money.

Viewed against the bewildering $44.4 billion long run fiasco of the B-2 bomber (which still doesn't work and neither the Pentagon nor the Air Force wants), the $28 billion marked for our becomingly named "intelligence community" (presided over by the murderously inept CIA), down to the perennial confrontations over tobacco subsidies (grotesquely enhanced by the hundreds of billions in overall farm subsidies gone largely and routinely into the wrong pockets), charges of the NEA being compromised by politics, and of "practicing censorship on a grand scale" wither as plain slander, and the mockery of its moribund $171.4 million appropriation offers little but comic relief. Short of taking a leaf from farm programs handing out taxpayer money to let fields lie fallow and paying writers not to write, sheer attrition may do it.

If the NEA massacre is not a matter of money, then what is it?

Beneath tabloid portrayals of the artist as layabout, as purveyor of drugs and obscenity, suicidal and sexually deviant but, above all, seditious, lurks the deeply ensconced fear of the artist for precisely what he is: the agent of change. From his proscription by Plato (rhymes with tomato, Senator) down to the Soviet grasp from the outset that he must be either shackled in its service or erased, or perhaps, in the less bloodthirsty American grain, he would simply shut up and go away if snubbed and ignored. "He's doing interviews and book tours and things that authors do. But there's no reason to have any special interest in him," bleated White House spokesman Marlin Fitzwater, shrugging off the appeal of a writer under death sentence by a distant Ayatollah, busied as he was touting a pusillanimous Administration whose President was being eulogized in a best-selling picture book by the family dog. But Salman Rushdie goes on writing, and Fitzwater sealing his contempt proclaiming "You *can* run and hide" doing things that authors do with his own anecdotal entry into the lists of the fifty thousand books published a year increasingly filled by political flacks and celebrities and "personalities" no one has ever heard of, ex-generals and ex-convicts and books, as Cyril Connolly observed just fifty years ago, on "how to achieve a cheap sentimental humanism at other people's expense." Ah, but a man's reach should exceed his grasp, or what's a First Amendment for? Then picture this: The projected novel *1945* opens in a Washington bedroom where a "beautiful and exotic" German spy (masquerading as a Swedish newspaper woman), working over the White House Chief of Staff, bites his shoulder "only minutes since their last lovemaking [*sic*] . . . and then kissed it better. . . . 'Such a book I could write,' " says she, and as "Suddenly the pouting sex kitten gave way to Diana the Huntress. She rolled onto him and somehow was sitting athwart his chest, her knees pinning his shoulders" leaving him panting and, as "she twined the fur on his chest," with "the movement of her fingers, which were no longer on his chest . . . suddenly wanting her very much. . . . She was truly an artist."

With no evidence that the author of this morsel sought NEA support for this venture into creative fiction, of those hundreds of manuscripts I read none, not one, descended to this level of trite vulgarity by Newt Gingrich tentatively aimed for the best-seller lists in the spring, when from over a thousand submissions for grants in poetry the NEA will award twenty-one, and those in creative writing will probably fare similarly. While funding support for such independent crusades as PEN's worldwide Freedom to

Write programs may pale before the sums paid lobbyists who actually help to write, for example, watered down versions of Congressional anti-pollution legislation, the business of America is, after all, business, and for good reasons the writer has been and remains an endagered species. That is our edge.

SPEECHES

THE ITEMS INCLUDED IN THIS section came relatively late in Gaddis's career, when after years of reticence he would come to speak in public about the conditions of writers in the U.S. and abroad. William Kennedy, who brought in Gaddis to speak at the Writers Institute in Albany, New York, recalls Gaddis's early reluctance: "As soon as [the Institute] was invented, I asked Gaddis to come and visit and speak, and he said, 'Absolutely, positively, no!' I didn't give up, and some years later, I tried again and his 'no' wasn't quite so resounding and then the following year he said, 'maybe,' and then one day, in 1990, he was talking to an Albany newspaperman, and he said, 'there is nothing more distressing or tiresome than a writer standing in front of an audience and reading his work' " (the Albany *Times Union,* April 2, 1990). Two days later, there was Bill Gaddis on stage at the Recital Hall at the university, not reading his work to the audience but reading from index cards why he didn't read his work to audiences" (transcript of excerpts from the New York State Author and Poet Award Ceremony honoring William Gaddis and Richard Howard, November 10, 1993).

A strategy typical of Gaddis, avoiding speaking by making a theme of avoidance, recurs in each of the four speeches printed here. In the first, on receiving the National Book Award for *J R,* his insistence that writers should be read rather than seen or heard made a nice contrast with the next speaker—Norman Mailer. With time, however, Gaddis accepted the responsibilities that came with recognition although he continued to take his creative irresponsibilities just as seriously. William Gass recounted the transformation at the May 1999 memorial service, from the same stage where Gaddis accepted that first NBA twenty-three years before: "the mysterious Mister Gaddis is actually seen in public, is elected to the Academy, earns a MacArthur, writes a book in less than twenty years. He must be slipping." A Lannan Foundation Lifetime Achievement Award would follow, and a 1993 Edith Wharton Citation of Merit as New York State Author. (Gaddis did not prepare formal speeches for either occasion and so they are not included here. A transcription of Gaddis's words accepting the New York State award does exist, however.)

ON RECEIVING THE NATIONAL
BOOK AWARD FOR *J R*

To list every one I owe a lasting debt in relation to the occasion for this award would go back a good many years, and keep us here all evening. I have simply got to trust in their awareness of my gratitude. At the very least though, I must of course thank the judges who have given J R this distinction.

After that, I feel like part of the vanishing breed that thinks a writer should be read and not heard, let alone seen. I think this is because there seems so often today to be a tendency to put the person in the place of his or her work, to turn the creative artist into a performing one, to find what a writer says about writing somehow more valid, or more real, than the writing itself.

In this regard, I was struck by something I read recently in a preface to a novel of Gorky's. "Before 1880," this editor noted—his name is F. D. Reeve—"before 1880, roughly, the main problem about being a writer was to keep writing well. By the end of the century, the main problem was to write well enough to establish or to maintain the position of being a writer."

If that provides a glimpse of a current dilemma, it seems to me the only way to keep writers writing well, or trying to write well, is to read what we write.

And if this reeks as a truism, we're back where we started, which may recommend it as a good place to stop.

HOW DOES THE STATE IMAGINE?
THE WILLING SUSPENSION
OF DISBELIEF

We who struggle to create fictions of various sorts, and with varying success, must regard the state with awe, for the state itself may be the grandest fiction to be concocted by man, barring only one.

The collision course on which we as writers frequently find ourselves with this Leviathan lies in the efforts of the state to preserve and protect its own imagined version of itself, confronted by the writer's individual imagined version of what the state—what life in the state, that is to say—could and should, or at least should not be.

Thus much of our fiction, going back well over a century, has been increasingly fueled by outrage or, at the least, by indignation. Curiously enough, this is often coupled with and even springs from the writer's perennially naive notion that through calling attention to inequities and abuses, hypocrisies and patent frauds, self-deceiving attitudes and self-defeating policies, these will be promptly corrected by a grateful public; but the state is the public's fiction, and gratitude is not its most prominent attribute.

In our work we are all familiar, overly familiar, with that injunction regarding the willing suspension of disbelief on the part of the reader, and here the great irony emerges: The more ingeniously, the more humanly and even the more comically, especially in the exaggeration of satire, we attempt to embrace reality—you might even say truth—the more vigorous the efforts of the state to flee from reality in fictions of such magnitude and audacity that we are swamped in admiration and dismay.

The most sweeping feat of the human imagination dwarfing even that of the state itself, where the state historically seeks refuge and in fact may well have been born, is that invisible realm of revealed wisdom, revealed truths, divine revelations. Expressed in extremes ranging from passive resistance to indiscriminate murder, this phenomenon overwhelms us today in all sorts of national regalia, speaking in tongues of every register, under the common name Fundamentalism. It is often hailed in laudatory terms of a religious awakening. It often, recalling its bloody forebears in the late Middle Ages, presents itself as a crusade.

There is no end to its variety, no end to its faces and their colors, no end to its mischief among Arabs and Jews, Hindus and Moslems, Moslems and Christians and all their offspring: Protestant, Catholic, Sunni, Shiite, Ashkenazim and Sephardim, Sikhs, Maronites, Melkites, Copts . . . each with its own divinely inspired conviction of what the state could and, at the cost of its very life, should be.

In armed conflicts that wither before the prospect of the nuclear war they invite, these voices rise from the pervasive fear of uncertainty in a primordial cry for higher authority, a cry for order and community, for having been put here on earth for some purpose, some vital place in some grand design. And according to their numbers, the urgency becomes one of whether this tumult will nourish the imagination of the state, and thus the state itself, or simply devour it.

When push comes to shove, the side with the feebler imagination goes down as, in Iran, the state went down with its tedious array of secret police, torture chambers, glittering weaponry and obtuse assistance from our own great Christian nation. In other words, the unbridled imagination of the true believer prevailed in its desperate need for absolutes which, as has been remarked elsewhere, should have been shot in the cradle.

There are, for example, many alive today in Russia who long for the days of Stalin.

Nikolai Gogol was literally consumed by his holy mission to save Russia. Tolstoy spent a long and busy lifetime at it, and Dostoevski's efforts barely got him off with his life. But it was the hands of Lenin that seized opportunity when last it came, to shape the imagination of the Leviathan we ponder today, where on a recent visit to his mausoleum in the Kremlin, one traveler observes the queue "drab, dogged, muttering. . . . But as it turns to face the tomb, a low ziggurat in red marble, it falls silent. People remove their hats, smooth down their hair. The odor of sanctity is suddenly intense and oppressive. This is the Holy Sepulchre of atheism. . . . The cult of Lenin seems to have stepped into some deep atavistic breach left open by Christianity in retreat. It appeals to the same spirit in which people wept in panic and trampled women and children to death at the funerals of the tsars and of Stalin himself. It is part of the hunt for God."

We in America, of course, have found him; and moreover, as you may gather from our present Administration, are putting him to good use. Almost half our population believes that he created man in his present form about ten thousand years ago. Three in four of us believe that Jesus is alive in heaven, and two-thirds that he must be accepted to gain eternal life, though barely more than half of us can name all four Gospels, and just under the other half can name none. Armed with these articles of faith, our vice president, sworn to uphold the constitutional separation of church and state, his walleye cocked on his party's presidential primary two years hence, is on his way to address a convocation whose popular leader states: "The idea that religion and politics don't mix was invented by the Devil to keep Christians from running their own country."

Meanwhile our president, enjoined by scripture to curb the aggressive instincts of the evil empire, justifies our massive military buildup with Jesus's words in the Gospel according to St. Luke, relieving him of the scriptures of more recent history and responsibility for history yet to be made, and earning him the credibility of 67 percent of our population.

As writers of fictions, we had seen dealing with the willing suspension of disbelief as our own particular province; but it is, we discover, the very ground of the imagination of the state in relieving its majority of the burden of responsibility for their own individual destinies. It's as though our one real weapon had been usurped; but we've no choice but to get on with it, to cling in our own fictions, in our own versions of the state, to what responsible intelligence, what individual life in the state that is to say, could and should be.

ON RECEIVING THE NATIONAL
BOOK AWARD FOR *A FROLIC*
OF HIS OWN

I'm glad this time that we're in the library, which is generally devoted to reading books rather than talking about them. I have in the past supported libraries. I've done a little on Long Island, "Support Your Public Library"; that's when my books were out of print, and I thought that was the one place you might see them. Now that they're back in print, I encourage people to go to the bookstore.

There was a man, a marvelous fellow, wrote a marvelous book, you may have heard this, his name was Amos Tutuola. He was a Nigerian. Twenty or thirty years ago, he wrote a marvelous book called *The Palm Wine Drinkerd*. His teacher thought he was quite intriguing and original, and sent the manuscript to Faber in London, who published it, sent him the customary ten copies, complementary author's copies, which he proceeded to get out on the street and try to sell. He happened into the big, large department store in Lagos, and here was his book. He was furious, and said, "This is my book, what are you doing with it? You're getting paid for it." Maybe we should all have to handle things like that instead of these book tours and signings and readings.

Again, I think one of the most depressing moments I have come across in a long time is when Salman Rushdie was trying to get in to see someone in the Administration, about, obviously, his own case, but on behalf of writers who were put in various levels of the position he was in, and none of the members of that pusillanimous administration would see him. He told Marlin Fitzwater, who said, "Oh, we just treated him like another writer on a book tour." Now, if that doesn't give you the blues, I don't know what will.

I'll read you something I wrote. I wrote it forty years ago, in my first novel, which was published forty years ago; so I'd written it before that, obviously. It's a man who's a painter, and his wife, who is very fond of the arts and is going to some sort of episode where she's going to meet an important poet, no offense, and he says: "This passion for wanting to meet the latest poet, shake hands with the latest novelist, get hold of the latest painter, devour, what is it, what is it they want from a man total that they didn't get from his work? What do they expect? What is there left of him when he's done his work? What's any artist but the dregs of his work? The human shambles that follows it around." And here I am this evening.

Julian Barnes, you will know from *Flaubert's Parrot*, he says, you expect something from me too, don't you? It's like that nowadays. People assume they own part of you, no matter how small an acquaintance. Well if you are reckless enough to write a book, just put your bank account, your medical records, and the state of your marriage irrevocably in the public domain. Flaubert disapproved. "The artist must manage to make posterity believe that he never existed," and I like that approach very much.

There was a justice, Oliver Wendell Holmes Jr., who decreed all his papers would be burned. He said, simply, I want to be known by the finished product. That is, his opinions and dissents. He said, how I got there is no one else's business, and I feel that way too; except that now the universities are interested in purchasing the so-called archives, so we begin to save every piece of trash that comes out of the typewriter, with that hope in mind. Some even end up here!

For reading, I think poets, obviously, they have a tradition of the troubador, of reading poetry aloud. So I would feel separate from that, in fiction; also, in nonfiction, someone who writes nonfiction obviously has some ideas that he's interested in communicating. Not the art of it, no offense, but artfully, if he can. But he has a program, an "agenda" is the word we use now. Some view of something to share, whereas a fiction writer, I think, is to me very much between the reader and the page, not between the reader and the writer.

I'm at a disadvantage in that area, because most of my work is with dialogue. You have to be a sort of an actor to get away with reading it aloud. I have heard Bill Gass read some of my work, and I must say he did a marvelous job. I read some of his aloud, and told the audience, "Wouldn't you rather have been alone at home, reading this lovely page, rather than have me spoil it for you by getting in the way of it?" Which is the way I felt about it.

At any rate, we go back to, I go back to take you back with me, to Marshall McLuhan, if we remember him. He said, distinguishing, remember all this business about the hot and cool media, and this is, what, twenty to thirty years ago. He said a hot medium, like television, has high definition in the sense that it is so well filled with data that the viewer need bring little to his participation besides passive reception. A cool medium, such as a book, on the other hand, has low definition in that it provides less information, leaving much of the experience to be filled in by the reader.

Cool media are high in participation, or completion, by the

audience. And I have always taken that to heart, that sometimes it can be a dangerous practice.

I'm not reader-friendly. I do ask something of the reader, and many reviewers say I ask too much; even some of them who like my work say, but it's work, it's difficult; and as I say, it's not reader-friendly.

Though I think it is, and I think that a reader gets satisfaction out of participating in, collaborating, if you will, with the writer, so that it ends up being between the reader and the page, without this whole world of giving readings. You read to children. Why did we invent the printing press? Why do we, why are we literate? Because of the pleasure of being all alone, with a book, is one of the greatest pleasures.

At any rate, an early review of my work made a point; the reviewer said, this was my first book forty years ago, "What is this book about? Mr. Gaddis doesn't say." And this is Norbert Wiener, if you remember him, on entropy. He says, "We are always fighting nature's tendency to degrade the organized, and to destroy the meaningful. The more probable a message, the less information it gives. Clichés, for example, are less illuminating than great poems."

And this is, I think, part of the danger that I see at work, though I won't name names. But I don't need to, because they make millions of dollars a year, books that are in McLuhan's realm, pretty warm media, requiring no effort whatsoever except some degree of literacy.

On the other hand, my second novel got this review by a man who shall be nameless for the moment, who wrote, "Recently a group of avant-garde critics have put forward the idea that a book should be made unreadable. This movement has manifest advantages. Being unreadable, a text repels reviewers, critics, anthologists, academic literati, and other parasitical forms of life." And then, on the notion that anybody can write a book, he says, "What then of the truly unreadable book? This surely must be in every man's reach, yet again, the answer is no. To produce an unreadable text, to sustain this foxy purpose over 726 pages, demands rare powers. Mr. Gaddis has them."

So it is, one does take a risk in asking something of the reader, because you don't know whose hands the book is going to fall into, and these are the risks you run. I must have gone on. It seems to me that we now increasingly, with this plague of the media in various forms, mainly, of course, television, the endless talking heads, confessionals, Montel Williams, I mean, really, the list is endless; and part of it is involved with the most deplorable human activities, which should never get off the printed page.

The others are so involved with creating, with personalities, with celebrity, with all of the transiency that is filling our lives. I like to think not that one should write so-called literature—a dangerous word; but something that will last is what I try to bend my efforts to. And everything seems to go against that. Everything now around us seems to be performance, performance, even this business of writers in performance. Well, I shouldn't bite the hand that's feeding me this evening here. I should also conclude by saying that if we get next to the Book-of-the-Month Club one way or the other, I've been trying for forty years, and here we are this evening, so I do appreciate their contribution here. That's enough of that, isn't it?

(*Audience applause*)

TRIBUTES

COMMISSIONED BY DENIS SCHECK and translated into German by Nikolaus Stingl, the first of these three late essays was broadcast on Dostoevski's 175th birthday on November 11, 1996, and published the same day in the *Frankfurter Allgemeine Zeitung*.

Dostoevski was of course a major influence on Gaddis, who considered him the greatest of the Russian novelists, if not the greatest novelist, period. The only fiction reading Gaddis ever gave was in the spring of 1991 for a local Wainscott, New York, library benefit. Asked to read from his own work, Gaddis demurred, and instead read a comic scene from *The Possessed*, which is also the main novel discussed in the German radio broadcast.

A second piece, titled "Mothers," was commissioned a month later, in December 1996, by the editor of the *Frankfurter Allgemeine*, Paul Ingendaay. The line "Men are what their mothers made them" is from a late essay by Emerson, "Fate." This sentence represents, for many readers of Emerson, an apparent turn away from a lifelong commitment to transcendentalism toward a more materialist outlook that would have resonated better with Gaddis.

Gaddis was too ill to deliver the tribute to Julian Schnabel, which was read at the American Academy of Arts in 1998.

DOSTOEVSKI

Although one would hardly classify the author of *Crime and Punishment*, *The Brothers Karamazov*, and *The Idiot* as a comic writer, in what may be the darkest of his novels steeped in murder, suicide, and madness, political conspiracy and despoiled innocence, Feodor Dostoevski found room in *The Possessed* for a scathingly comic portrait of Turgenev, a delicious parody of German romanticism, even a passing glimpse of the death of an American who has left his bones to science and "his skin to be made into a drum, so that the American national hymn might be beaten upon it day and night." At every opportunity, humor takes the measure of the disharmony, incongruity, and absurdity that mark the intrusion of the irrational in the turmoil of human affairs.

The devil, as they say, is in the details: in an early scene establishing two of the novel's major characters, the wealthy, imperious Varvara Petrovna Stavrogin, besieged on all sides by aimless lives and souls adrift in confusion and wrong turns, bursts in upon her hapless protégé, the aging aesthete Stepan Verhovensky, with "You're alone; I'm glad; I can't endure your friends. How you do smoke! What an atmosphere! You haven't finished your morning tea and it's nearly twelve o'clock. It's your idea of bliss—disorder! You take pleasure in dirt. What's that torn paper on the floor?" she descends in a torrent of abuse. "Open the window, the casement, the doors, fling everything wide open. And we'll go into the drawing room. I've come to you on a matter of importance . . ." and once there, "You've a wretched drawing room," she comes on, "You must have it repapered. Didn't I send a paperhanger to you with patterns? Why didn't you choose one? Sit down and listen."

The demon she pursues with such vengeance is, of course, this disorder, no less an obsession of hers than it had become with Dostoevski himself.

Deep into middle age, racked by illness, poverty, and debt, and estranged from his mother country where his radical youth, prison, and Siberia lay behind him, he had settled in Dresden to write this novel indicting that youthful vision of a socialist utopia with the ruinous disorder and the cult of Nihilism that had followed in its wake.

While radical youth turning conservative with age is common enough, there was nothing commonplace about Dostoevski's conversion. He pursued it as passionately as the gambling fever which haunted his life, a life which he now found unbearable at the mercies of a disorderly universe, a disorder threatening the very foundations of a Russia grounded in the Absolutes of the Orthodox Church and the hand of an inscrutable God where he sought refuge.

Hailed as a prophet of the revolutionary upheavals that convulsed Russia in 1905–6 and again in 1917, Dostoevski may be seen today in the ever widening prophetic terms of our own time, where authoritarian government and the imposition of law and order carry the seeds of fascism, where fundamentalism clothed in revealed religion battles the irrational in the collision between a world of Absolutes and a contingent universe embracing difference and discontinuity, contradiction, discord, ambiguity, irony and paradox, perversity, opacity, anarchy and chaos in an academic discipline dignified with the Greek label *aporia*, the realm with which Dostoevski grappled with all the frantic energies of the memorable characters he created.

"It's your idea of bliss—disorder!" Varvara Petrovna had

burst out in her relentless battle against the demon being hatched by sloth and carelessness wherever she looked, manipulating the lives around her from her tyranny of wealth like that "matter of importance" bringing her to the door of her hapless protégé. "This happy thought came to me in Switzerland," she explained, informing him of her "arranging" his marriage to a twenty-year-old girl with the same intensity she'd brought to redecorating his wretched drawing room, till all of her efforts to impose order would melt into the general disorder surrounding her, where like marriage and wallpaper, everything would eventually equal everything else in an ultimate vision of chaos, and the decay of meaning in the creeping entropy slowly silencing all, leaving her at last to strike out with "You're a fool, a fool! You're all ungrateful fools. Give me my umbrella!"

MOTHERS

When Ralph Waldo Emerson informed—or rather, perhaps, warned us—that we are what our mothers made us, we might dismiss it as received opinion and let it go at that, like the broken clock which is right twice a day, like the self-evident answer contained in Freud's oft-quoted query "What do women want?" when, as nature's handmaid, she must want what nature wants which is, quite simply, More. But which woman? Whose mother, Emerson's? A woman so in thrall to religion that we confront another dead end; or Freud's? or even one's own, even mine, offering an opportune bit of wisdom to those of us engaged in the creative arts, where paranoia is almost an occupational hazard: "Bill, just try to remember," she said, "there is much more stupidity than there is malice in the world," an observation lavish with possibilities recalling Anatole France finding the fool more dangerous than the rogue because "the rogue does at least take a rest sometimes, the fool never."

This is hardly to see stupidity and malice as mutually exclusive: look at your morning paper, where their combined forces explode exponentially (women and children first) from Bosnia to Belfast, unlike the international "intelligence community" so self-contained in its malice-free exercises that it generally ensnares only its own dubious cast of players. Of further importance is the distinction between stupidity and ignorance, since ignorance is educable, while stupidity's self-serving mission is the cultivation and exploitation of ignorance, as politicians are keenly aware.

How, then, might Emerson's mother have seen herself stumbling upon Thomas Carlyle's vision of her son as a "hoary-headed and toothless baboon"? Or Freud's, in the gross unlikelihood of her reading the *Catholic World*'s review of her son's book *Moses and Monotheism* as "poorly written, full of repetitions . . . and spoiled by the author's atheistic bias and his flimsy psychoanalytic fancies"? Goethe's *Wilhelm Meister* dismissed as "sheer nonsense" by the *Edinburgh Review* and, a good century later, the hero of Saul Bellow's *Dangling Man* ridiculed as a "pharisaical stinker" in *Time* magazine, John Barth's *The End of the Road* recommended by *Kirkus Reviews* "for those schooled in the waste matter of the body and the mind," and William Faulkner's *Absalom, Absalom!* shrugged off as the "final blowup of what was once a remarkable, if minor, talent" by *The New Yorker* magazine where, just forty years later, "a group of avant-garde critics has put forward the idea that books *should* be made unreadable. This movement has manifest advantages. Being unreadable, the text repels reviewers, critics, anthologists, academic literati, and other parasitical forms of life," indicting the author of the novel *J R* wherein "to produce an unreadable text, to sustain this foxy purpose over 726 pages, demands rare powers. Mr. Gaddis has them."

"You're a fool, a fool!" the distraught mother of Dostoevski's ill-fated hero Nikolay Stavrogin cries out at the "parasitical forms of life" surrounding her. "You're all ungrateful fools. Give me my umbrella!"

JULIAN SCHNABEL

It is a great pleasure and a great privilege to introduce the artist Julian Schnabel on the occasion of his receiving the Lifetime Achievement Award from the Guild Hall Academy of the Arts.

It is almost as equally painful for me to be unable to deliver this introduction myself this evening, but I am sure you will welcome the more melifluous tones of our colleague Sidney Lumet doing the honors and lending my own mundane observations a taste of drama.

We are living today in the market-driven Age of Imitation predicted by Walter Benjamin in which art is produced to be imitated, and where frequently enough we remember who did it last rather than who did it first.

We are living today in an Age of Entertainment shaped and controlled by the media in which time is shattered with all the hype, speed, and moral delinquency needed to reduce anything to trivia, as you may have seen in the television commercial featuring car wreck dummies singing the "Ode to Joy," suggesting that if we cannot rise to the artistic levels of Beethoven and Schiller, perhaps we can bring them down to ours.

We are living in an Age of Information, enlisting all values under its banner so indescriminately that it has already supplied our children's overflowing cornucopia of miseries with a new category called ADD, signifying Attention Deficit Disorder. Have you seen the great new Jackson Pollack retrospective at the Museum of Modern Art? No, I saw it on television. . . .

Must we learn again the simple, forthright experience of actually seeing a painting?

This may in fact be an essential aspect of the work of Julian Schnabel—painting on wood, on broken crockery, on the paint itself—demanding that we look, and look again, that we move forward from the American tradition of seeing art as decoration, as the safe refuge promised by *The New York Times* section labeled "Arts and Leisure," equating one with the other and thus putting a fine spin on the oxymoron in fashionable use on all sides today. In his relentless search for Authenticity, the Artist works to please himself in a constant process of Discovery through the very experience of the making of Art, and then seeking opportunities for it to prevail. Traveling abroad, he may encounter other cultural versions of himself, or as Julian Schnabel did in reviving the long-abandoned wreckage of the Cuartel del Carmen in Seville with a battle standard painted IDIOTA, opening himself to a Discovery in the past, in history, even in time itself. Nearer home, do his gigantic paintings on old Army tarpaulins dragged through the dirt open new avenues for Discovery in our own culture, and ask us to look again? I think so.

And finally here before you is the man himself: what you see is what you get, a man of extraordinary generosity, father of five assorted children devoted to one another and to their mothers, and to this man who has said from the start that he would trade places with no one, a lasting and a loyal friend, and the twinkle of an eye.

A P P E N D I X :
P R O J E C T S U M M A R Y A N D
W O R K I N G P A P E R S
F O R " A G A P Ē A G A P E :
T H E S E C R E T H I S T O R Y O F T H E
P L A Y E R P I A N O "

SUMMARY NOTES ON THE WORK IN PROGRESS

AT VARIOUS STAGES IN HIS CAREER, Gaddis used the title *Agapē Agape* for various projects: it is the history of mechanization and the arts that Gibbs works on, to little avail, in *J R*; it is Gaddis's own projected history of the player piano, worked on at intervals; and it became, finally, the title of his final fiction, a novella that condensed half a century's research into eighty-four manuscript pages. The title's first appearance is in the "Summary" written for his agent when Gaddis tried selling the player piano project in the early sixties. Although he had already published the "Stop Player" piece in *The Atlantic Monthly* and he had on hand numerous essay drafts and notes, the "Summary" is the first coherent statement of the project and the first time, not coincidentally, that the word "entropy" appears in his papers.

AGAPĒ AGAPE:
THE SECRET HISTORY OF THE PLAYER PIANO

Summary notes on the work in progress, to run to about fifty thousand words.

Agapē Agape is a satirical celebration of the conquest of technology and of the place of art and the artist in a technological democracy. As "The Secret History of the Player Piano," it pursues America's growth in terms of the evolution of the programming and organizational aspects of mechanization in industry and science, education, crime, sociology and leisure and the arts, between 1876 and 1929. That half century embraced the development, dominion and decline of the player piano, which at once anticipated—and, only slightly magnified, may appear to have brought about—both the patterned structure of modern technology and the successful democratization of the arts in America. In brief, the player is credited with introducing (1) punched-roll programming of "information," which is the basis of modern automation communications and control systems, and (2) the possibility of "creative participation" in artistic endeavor, at a time when leisure was becoming available to those with the desire but neither the skills nor talent for such expression.

In this study, the descent of technology is briefly traced back to European automata born of the decadent sequence of leisure's decline to boredom's demand for entertainment. And while response to the ensuing surge of industrial mechanization in England ranged from the Luddite riots (1811) to William Morris at his loom and Butler's ban on machines in his utopian *Erewhon* (1872), nothing was safe from or sacred to the mechanical inventiveness and applied practicality of late nineteenth-century America, where the player was to have its wide success.

Here, shortages of both goods and skilled labor and the daily feats of science and mechanization combined to foster a criterion of usefulness and the doctrine of progress. Further, the obsession with success, born of equal opportunity and bred by the self-made man's contempt for failure, projected a parochial confidence in the evolution of this best of all possible worlds, the militant paradox compounded of free will, moral choice, and determinism, still reflected in our insanity laws, which was admirably posed by the player piano. The fundamental concern of this study, and the source of our present dilemma, is the application of systems designed to accomplish tangible and predetermined ends, to such intangible goals as those of the arts which are determined only in their accomplishment, and concern the essence and eternal question of being. The real tyranny of technology lies in the fact that its impressive successes in its own areas encourage its intrusion into areas where such success is not only impossible but absurd; and just as the original design and even purpose of a product may be lost and forgotten as it takes its shape in terms of the capability of the machine which produces it, so in areas where technological progress has no relevance, and where technology as a means has no competence, it becomes an end in itself to the exclusion, the alienation, and at last the utter loss of aspirations to which it had never really pretended.

But such is logic, and only satire can project the pathos of a society at the peak of its development seeking, as the spinster pokes under her bed, to discover and define its National Goals, a quandry already evident in the career of the player as it evolved into the twentieth century to become more fool- and artist-proof, and thereby to demonstrate that the illusion of intimacy and proficiency is but the first step toward alienation.

For mechanization itself was not that era's real contribution to our modern technology, but rather the related but more pervasive principle of organization and programming manifest today in the anxious concern with patterns in automation and cybernetics, mathematics and physics, sociology, game theory, and, finally, genetics. These enterprises are detailed in *Agapē Agape* as they derive from that prime goal of applied science—the elimination of failure through analysis, measurement, and prediction—which even in its crude mechanistic stages proved so attractive a promise to industry that production patterns dictated by the machine were soon shaping corresponding patterns of uniformity elsewhere.

As both a source and an issue of the alienation of skills in work and in leisure, the career of the player paralleled the zeal for order and patriotic proclivities for standardization and programming contributed by McCormick (patents), Rockefeller (industry), Woolworth (merchandising), Eastman (photography), Morgan (credit), Ford (assembly line, plant police), Pullman (model town), Mary Baker Eddy (applied ontology), Taylor (time studies), Watson (behaviorism), Sanger (sex), &c., &c., as they are detailed in this chronicle. Yet while the player's development, juxtaposed with these careers, illuminated the thesis that "organization breeds more organization," it also signified, on the broader canvas of industrial democracy, the limitations of their achievements betrayed by their frequent and awkward gestures toward the arts. It signified the element which is missing when "You push the button—We do the rest" in the areas of the arts where truth and error are interdependent possibilities in the search for unpredetermined perfection. It was that element of loss and incompleteness, of unresolved estrangement from another self who could do more in just those erratic areas, which the player appeared to provide painlessly even as it programmed its extinction.

The almost total range of current and forecast capabilities of automation, cybernetics, and computers, which are duly explored in this study, need be noted here in a single detail helpful to grasping the final analogy.

The "best of all possible worlds" (what the NAM calls the "Golden Tomorrow") is granted here as one in which science "will embrace the social dynamics of man [and] will deal with the patterns, techniques, and structure of collectivisation under the comprehensive principle of organization set in motion on a universal scale by the machine."* When we note that a chief element in dealing with information programming in modern communications and control systems is that of entropy, the measurement of chaos or disorder which constantly threatens flawless functioning of the system, the analogy of the artist's threat to the social fabric becomes obvious, and the "scientific" case for order demanding his elimination is made clear.

---

*R. Seidenberg, *Posthistoric Man.*

PLAYER PIANO CHRONOLOGY
TO 1929

AT HIS DEATH, Gaddis left innumerable uncollected news items and "hundreds" of further "clippings, outlines, vast number of notes, drafts of early pages" intended for the player piano history. An American counterpart to Walter Benjamin's unfinished "Arcades" project, or—better still—a prize contribution to the still evolving "Dead Media" project initiated on the Internet by cyberpunk novelist Bruce Sterling (a compilation running from Klieg light spectacles to eight-track tape players and superseded software platforms), these notes show Gaddis working a rich vein of twentieth-century material culture. Although only a fraction can be reproduced here, the notes nonetheless offer numerous points of contact with the fiction and a sense of a project that Gaddis worked on all his writing life, one that preceded the publication of *The Recognitions*. No attempt is made here to indicate differences in typewriter font or notes written by hand, in a hand that changes over the course of fifty years. Newspaper and book clippings are identified, however.

Long before video killed the radio star, radio itself had done its bit to obviate the player piano—and this was at the very moment in the mid-1920s when the production of automatic players had itself overtaken the production of traditional, nonmechanical pianos. It is now well known in contemporary media studies that a new medium by its own success often creates the conditions for its demise—even as the elaborate settings in nineteenth-century novels created in readers a sensibility and desire for visual detail that only film would satisfy, later on. The nineteenth-century inventor John McTammany dreamed that his player would be, one day, "the only piano in evidence." In the event, as Gaddis notes, its success almost killed the entire piano industry by creating a generation of listeners unable to play by hand and—after radio—no longer in need of the bulky player mechanism. The traditional industry did revive, but only with radio's help, since (with the decline of domestic performances) radio's broadcasts were able to create in a new generation of listeners a renewed desire to play the songs themselves.

1731

Justinian Morse British "an organ which any person, without any musical skill whatsoever, can learn to play exactly and tastefully in an hour's time."

Vaucanson, the famous automation maker of Paris, pierced cylinder for flowered-silk weaving in producing mechanical Music.

1804

Jacquard's punch-card loom.

1811–15

Luddites

Nov. 24, **1859**, whole edition of 1,250 copies exhausted on day of issue: "On the Origin of Species by Means of Natural Selection, or the Preservation of Favoured Races in the Struggle for Life."

Mrs. Eddy: "In the nineteenth century I affix for all time the word *Science* to *Christianity*; and *error* to *personal sense*; and call the world to battle on this issue."

1870–71

The Birth of Tragedy appeared.

Player piano. Mechanical device for reproducing music can be traced back centuries; the principles of pneumatics (controlled air pressure) were successfully used in the construction of the tubular pneumatic actions of organs during the Middle Ages. Through the hand organ and barrel organ we find the *Antifunal* (Antiphonal) constructed in England—a minimal advance; but in the last half of the nineteenth century development was rapid. In **1863**, Fourneaux, a Frenchman, constructed an apparatus with a pneumatic device for actuating the keys of the piano which he called the Pianista. This was, strictly speaking, a *piano player* which could be added to the piano externally. This device had all the disadvantages of the barrel organ and was also turned by a crank; its precursor was probably the *Organette*. Other European experiments were made in England and in France by Morse, Seyere, Pain, and Pape.

John McTammany, a native of England, came to the United States early in life with his parents and settled in the Middle West, where he found employment as a mechanic in a plant producing reading machines. His two interests were machines and music.

1863

Fourneaux's Pianista: fingers pressed on keyboard by pneumatic action through a perforated cardboard; exhibited at Philadelphia Exposition, **1876**; also on exhibit was an electric organ made by Henry Schmock of Philadelphia. This organ used a music sheet of double width, slots of long notes being divided into half the length of the slot, the other half of the slot coming adjacent; the advantage of this scheme was that the paper was not weakened by a very long slot. The organ involved two sets of electric connections which made it impracticable for home use in the era of gas lighting.

1876

Bell exhibits telephone.

Mrs. Eddy and "a few of her students formed the Christian Science Association."

Wild Bill Hickock shot dead in Deadwood, S.D.

1872

Erewhon published.

1875

Mrs. Eddy published *Science and Health*—Hegel, plagiary.

1876–78

J. Willard Gibbs.

From a study of the values of commodity output in the eight census years between 1869 and 1919 we find the following products appearing for the first time—or becoming economically important enough to be listed as separate categories for the first time—in these years:

> paper patterns
> window shades and fixtures
> porcelain electrical supplies
> telephone apparatus
> adding machines, cash registers and parts and all other calculating
> machines
> chemical fire extinguishers
> bathtubs, lavatories, and sinks

[clipping]

1879

F. W. Woolworth opened his first 5¢ store, Utica, N.Y.

Offenbach dying, to his producer: "Make haste, make haste to mount my piece . . . I am in a hurry and have only one wish in the world"—to see the premier of his work. Died 5 Oct 1880; *Tales of Hoffmann* not produced till 10 Feb 1881. Act I ➤ about Spalanzani, who makes marvelous mechanical dolls, passes one off as his daughter and fools Hoffmann into falling in love with it (in Act III a girl sings herself to death).

1881

Higginson forms Boston Symphony Orchestra.

1887

Jack London born in San Francisco.

R. W. Emerson: "Society has played out its last stake; it is checkmated. Young men have no hope. Adults stand like day-laborers idle in the streets. None calleth us to labor. The old wear no crown of warm life on their grey hairs. The present generation is bankrupt of principles and hope, as of property. I see that man is not what man should be. He is a treadle of a wheel. He is the tassel of the apron-string of society. He is a money-chest. He is the servant of his belly. This is the causal bankruptcy, this the cruel oppression, that the ideal should serve the actual, that the head should serve the feet. . . ."

Nobel patented blasting gelatin (**1876**); nitroglycerin in smokeless powder (**1889**).

(Dynamite, **1862**.)

Custer massacre "made war again exciting."

McTammany got idea of the player piano during the Civil War in which he fought, so it was that the player ". . . came into being amid the stress and struggle of war during the rattle of musketry, clash of steel and din of battle" where it sprang up as a "pure white lily."
  (*History of the Player* by John McTammany)

McTammany took out patents for his devices, and found that only two patents had been issued for anything approaching similarity; those were by Hunt and Bradish, and by Van Dusen. Van Dusen admitted, upon investigation, that McTammany had anticipated him by a couple of years. . . .

1850–91

Rise and domestic triumph of American-made pianos: though practically identical with piano players of a century later, these early productions aroused little interest among genteel families unready for mechanical music; but the masses, the people who throng the streets, were ready, and thus the invention and success in the nineteenth century of street piano. Battle against "monopoly of the piano by the upper 10,000 as a fraud on the lower ten millions" by Joseph P. Hale whose "pianos had all the parts of any other pianos, therefore they must be just as good" and though "no great works of art, they were better than the pianists who were to play them—or the music they were destined to bring forth."

"And speaking of the player piano back in the hey-day of popularity of that instrument, we are reminded to mention that Fred H. Patton, who once held a key position with the old Autopiano Co., a division of the Kohler Industries, and was well known as a baritone soloist, is now located in East Lansing, Michigan, where he is a successful voice teacher. . . ."

("Is the Player Piano Coming Back?" *Music Dealer*, volume 4, March 1950, page 94)

1870–90

Pianos multiplied 1.6 times as fast as people.

(Following McTammany) "Inventions by Merritt Gally and by Bishop & Downe of England in **1881** and **1883** respectively, but these had no permanent effect on the development of the player piano, although they created sensations at the time."

"Central Park in Manhattan opened its [bicycle] paths in **1887** and women flocked to its winding trails . . . when the American woman adapted herself to the changes of the times (and even resorted to 'bloomers' as one means of facilitating her enjoyment of the sporting life), cycling became an issue for public discussion . . . a cycling mania swept rapidly throughout the country, and manufacturers of bicycles were overwhelmed with orders as prices descended to the $30 and $50 bracket."

1884

Freud told by Breuer of hysteria case cured "by getting the patient to recollect in a state of hypnosis the circumstances of their origin and to express the emotions accompanying this."

Panic in N.Y.

1885

First electric street railway in U.S. opened in Baltimore.

Mark Twain markets Ulysses S. Grant's book *Memoirs*, which yields $450,000.

"*Pneumatic and Electric Models*. In **1886** a wind motor with slide valves which opened and closed ports to pneumatic motors was invented by G.B. Kelly. This became exceedingly popular, and upon expiration of the patent it was adopted throughout the world."

Samuel Butler published *Luck or Cunning?*, continuing his dissent with Darwin: D.'s "natural selection" seemed to B. to "remove all idea of purpose from the universe," and to depend on the occurrence of variations, or "spots," whose appearance it left totally unexplained. Against this view, he maintained that variation was due, not to "luck," but to the striving (or "cunning") of the individual in adapting itself to its environment, and handed on by the inheritance of "unconscious memory" or "habit."

After rather high living, McTammany lost claims and suits in the yr **1888**, and apparently spent the rest of his years poor, in litigations. The justification of McTammy's claim, that his was the earliest revelation concerning the wonders of the player, cannot be argued now. But his account of its inception, written "in the shade of death" in the military hospital at Noroton Heights, Conn. while the constable in Stamford was taking his small Organette plant out into the streets for confiscation, is among the most devotional pieces of writing since Thoreau's *Walden*.

Sir Arthur Sullivan to Edison, terrified at the thought that so much hideous and bad music may be put on records forever.

McTammy still maintains himself as the originator of the player; and the player like Christ coming to the earth, not known by his own. And that it will someday be "the only piano in evidence."

In final litigations: "I was sorry that I was dying with inventions on my brain that would have blessed mankind could I have lived to develop them."

Nietzsche breaks with Wagner holding W.'s art as "nothing more than the dope required by a decadent generation."

Cabinet player piano presented to Anton Seidl, Wagnerian conductor of Met, his praise of it commercialized, he put it in attic and made unkind remarks about it in private.

1889

At Paris World's Fair, first automobile (a Benz) exhibited.
>   biological products
>   fountain pens
>   bicycles
>   typewriters and parts
>   polished wire glass and all other building glass
>   [clipping]

Nietzsche's breakdown and sister's forgery.

The gentleman of leisure was not yet extinct, but in **1896** he represented a small and diminishing species. The old aristocracy had begun to yield

to the importunate big moneymaker from the West . . . Pittsburgh . . .
the pursuit of power absorbs them completely. The game exacted un-
remitting vigilance. They had little or no time for leisure. When they
spared time leisure was apt to make them restless. One could spend
money, but how did one kill time? So leisure, as an end in itself, as a way
of life, was going out of fashion. It was coming to seem discreditable, ef-
fete, almost decadent.

Bryan to "20 thousand yelling, cursing, shouting men": "you shall not
press down upon the brow of labor this crown of thorns, you shall not
crucify mankind upon a cross of gold."

Many of the piano makers of the day stoutly resisted any plans to put
players inside their instruments. To them a piano that bulged in odd
places because it was pregnant with machinery was an affront to the aesthetic senses, and not to be tolerated. Nevertheless, the buying public
very soon made its decision—against the separate cabinets and for the
pregnant pianos.

[clipping]

1897

Thorndike with chickens in James's cellar studying their intelligence.

St. Crane in England, where he finds O. Wilde a "mildewed chump."

Richard Corey.

1899

78,073 typewriters manufactured (bringing women into world of affairs
for first time).

Thorndike on transfer of acquired abilities from one area to another.

Conspicuous leisure, vicarious leisure in the women, daughters of the
family, according to Veblen, already preoccupied with womens' corsets,
"in economic theory, substantially a mutilation, undergone for the pur-

pose of lowering the subject's vitality and rendering her permanently and obviously unfit for work."

At the piano; stays unlaced to pump?

> phonograph needles
> gasoline
> incandescent lamps
> phonographs and dictating machines
> passenger cars
> motorcycles
>
> [clipping]

Frank Norris *McTeague—Story of San Francisco* shows: "attitude which exalts subject matter over art & regards life as more real the closer man comes to the level of the brute. Naturalism has had a great appeal in America because it enables the writer and his reader to conform to the ideal of manliness evolved by the social and industrial frontier...."

"general democratic craving to be ruled by the pretenses of the Joneses, American homes at the end of the 19th century harboured a million pianos nobody could play to amount to anything."

1900

Sister Carrie arrives Chicago.

Kipling to visit Mark Twain that summer.

Carrie Nation began raiding saloons w hatchet.

St. Crane in England unable to leave, writing in bed.

Dreiser's *Sister Carrie* published and suppressed (by Doubleday): "What made *Sstr Carrie* the shocker of its day, postponing the author's success, was that it depicted a woman who was a success, without regard to the respectability of her means. This was un-American."

Meanwhile brother (entertainer) Paul Dreiser's success with *My Gal Sal*, on the Bowery.

"America is good enough for me," remarked J. Pierpont Morgan a few days ago. Whenever he doesn't like it, he can give it back to us.
(Wm. Jennings Bryan, "The Commoner")

Wright Bros. built their first large glider (bicycle shop) in **1903**; 9 days later, flew powerdriven plane at Kitty Hawk, N.C.; world's awareness that human flight possible not till **1908**.

Six-day (60-hr.) week common; golf a diversion of the rich; less than 8000 cars in U.S. and less than 10 miles of concrete road.

Nietzsche dies.

1901

Wm. Sydney Porter released from Fed. Penitentiary, Columbus, Ohio, and started selling stories under name O Henry.

Theodore Roosevelt scandal has Booker T. Washington to lunch.

Holmes made Supreme Court Justice **1902**.

Trouble with music publishers in London, who didn't want their music vulgarized (rather than popularized, as player makers would say) attempted to get injunctions forbidding their playing on rolls.

Players doing well in England, France, but not Vienna, where everyone plays an instrument, so that "mechanical music" is disapproved—"Aber es kommt nicht von Herz."

The *Fliegende Blaetter*, in Munich: a cartoon of a heavy-footed German restaurant helper seated at a piano player. The hotel manager is speaking: "There come the delegates to the music teacher's convention. Tell John to play something by Chopin."

Aeolian was 5,000 behind in orders in Pittsburgh.

One British Company (J. G. Murdoch & Co. Ltd.) quoted as saying there were over a million useless pianos in Britain. Trade will come, they are sure.

Another manufacturer felt that the British public liked to spend its money, but expected a substantial return. "Buyers will feel that they are getting value for their money," he said, commenting on the elaborate structure of the player, "and the intimation that a player contains so many rows of pneumatic cylinders, or chambers; so many rows of pistons and valves, and so many pallets, will reconcile a buyer to the cost of the instrument."

Hearst sends J. London to cover Boer War.

1903

Samuel P. Langley's flying machine crashed.

Ford Motor Co. organized.

Wm. James had found freedom "to be a certain looseness in the conjunction of things, so that what the future shall be is not made inevitable by past history and present form; freedom or chance corresponds to Darwin's 'spontaneous variations' (i.e., spots, v. Butler); it is what saves history from being mere repetition."

Gordon on drugs as aesthetic experience.

And then, as if in answer to Tremaine's prayer for player piano prestige, a German manufacturer, Edwin Welte, of Freiburg im Breisgau, came up with an idea that gave the entire burgeoning industry a further boost. In those early days all player piano rolls were made by a purely mechanical process. Welte's notion was to use the actual playing of a pianist to create the master roll. A special piano was made with electrical contacts under each key.

[clipping]

1904

Thorndike publishes first handbook on measurement in the social sciences.

260,000 pianos built; 252,000 uprights; 7,000 grands; 1,000 plyrs.
    pneumatic tires and tubes for automobiles
    business motor vehicles—buses, sightseeing wagons, trailers, etc.

John Dewey comes to join philosophy department at Columbia: revolutionizes education reflecting industrial revolution and development of democracy.

Veblen—theory of business enterprise.

Headline: A CHILD CAN OPERATE IT.

Chinese, Prince Pu Lun, visiting World's Fair in St. Louis, enthusiastic; gives man who plays him recital 2 vases, $2,000. Buys Starr upright and Cecilian player, to be shipped "to the Forbidden City in the Chinese capital"; order written on royal parchment, accompanied by spot cash.

Besides Prince Po, there were 12,804,615 paid admissions at the Exposition, most of whom had not made it to Glasgow in 1901, and were seeing players for the first time.

The Welte Company moved quickly to get down on perforated rolls a number of short pieces played by some of the most famous pianists of the day. With an eye on history they also persuaded various composers—Grieg, Debussy, Saint-Saens, Scriabin, Richard Strauss, Faure, Glazunov, Leoncavallo, Ravel, and others—to record.
    [clipping]

Finley Peter Dunne, "Mr. Dooley," the only man of letters whom Henry James expressed a wish to meet on his return to the U.S.

New York is Greatest Player Town in the World (headline): 20 percent of total **1906** sales were players. Also doing well in Mexico.

Group banded together in the District of Columbia, called itself the Association of Automatic Piano Players, and adopted a constitution which gave as its object the securing "for the players educational advantages insuring increased pleasure and profit from Automatic Pianos." Article 4, concerning officers, provided that "no two officers of such committee shall be owners of the same make of player."

If the repair men are troubled, the companies are immediately ready with books on their machines.

Upton Sinclair, *The Jungle*, described the mechanization of pig slaughtering and Pure Food Bill came up for discussion in Congress, apparently all foods adulterated, chemically treated for color, &c.

M. Gorky comes to U.S. to publicize the Russian revolution, all goes swimmingly until discovered that woman with him not his wife: U.S. rose up against him: out he went.

Russell Sage died "the village skinflint writ large": his fortune destined by his widow for humanitarian causes.

Henry Adams's *Education* privately printed.

1907

Three Weeks published England, in other countries soon after:
". . . She bent over and kissed him, and smoothed his cheek with her velvet cheek, she moved so that his curly lashes might touch her bare neck, and at last she slipped from under him and laid his head gently down upon the pillows. Then a madness of tender caressing seized her. She purred as a tiger might have done, while she undulated like a snake. She touched him with her fingertips, she kissed his throat, his wrists, the palms of his hands, his eyelids, his hair. Strange subtle kisses, unlike the kisses of women. And often, between her purrings she murmured love-words in some fierce language of her own, brushing his ears and his eyes with her lips the while. And through it all Paul slept on, the Eastern perfume in the air drugging his senses. . . ."

Abusive letters, tiger skins, and "Would you like to sin / with Elinor Glyn / on a tiger skin? / Or would you prefer / to err / with her / on some other fur?"

Autumn: Mrs. Glyn, age 42, sailed for America on *Lusitania* (its first trip to N.Y.): purple overcoat purple toque purple chiffon veil and 60 pairs of high-heeled shoes.

In N.Y. she talked with some boxers: "I felt obliged to ask them if they minded at all having their heads smashed in, and black eyes, and if they felt nervous ever—and the little colored gentleman grinned and said he only felt nervous over the money of the thing! He was not anxious about the art or fame! He just wanted to win. Is not that an extraordinary point of view, Mama, *to win*? It is the national motto, it seems, *how* does not matter so much and that is what makes them so splendidly successful, and that is what the other nations who play games with them don't understand. . . ."

Oberlin adds physics to degree requirements.

Nobel Prize (to R. Kipling): "the person who shall have produced in the field of literature the most distinguished work of an idealist tendency."

Christmas holidays: Glyn, who'd written indecent novel called *Three Weeks,* called on Mark Twain, at 72 with income of $90,000 a yr, his own an Alger-like democracy success story, considered his life an American failure, looked at U.S. at dawning of 20th century filled with abhorrence, saw U.S. going way Rome had gone, man a useless thought in a blind mechanism universe: U.S. material prosperity produced conditions that debased morals, &c., acid contempt on U.S. passion for wealth.

James feted in Britain. *Pragmatism* best-seller practically: "the cash value of truth."

"The meaning of any idea whatsoever can be found ultimately in nothing save the succession of experiential consequences it leads through and to . . . against all finalities, staticisms and completenesses."

Peirce bequeathed the word pragmatism to James & Dewey, renaming his own doctrine "Pragmaticism," a term "ugly enough to be safe from kidnapers."

James-Dewey approach part of a later 19th century trend toward anti-intellectualism distorting Peirce, and criticized as having "no standards for truth other than practical material results": this, at any rate, their popular effect.

1908

American Piano Co. organized.

The Electrelle Co. makes one of first electric-operated machines, abolishing foot pumping—great step—invented by a Philadelphian.

American women smoked in their homes, it was known, never in public, and N.Y.C. passed a law against it.

Society collapsed with the death of Mrs. Astor.

Mrs. Eddy, age 87, established *Christian Science Monitor.*

H. Ford introduces Model T.

Freud, Jung, Stekel, Adler, Brill, Ferenczi hold first International Congress of Psycho-Analysis.

Movements to bar coin machines in some cities. N.Y., Cheyenne permitted them, though Lynn, Mass., where music had never been allowed in public places, did not; Indiana forbids them; Butte, Mont., was considering passing an ordinance; Kansas City, somewhat west of Lynn, prohibited music in saloons only; Jackson, Miss., didn't care; Souix Falls kept them out of saloons, to make such places less attractive.

Owners of Pianolas: Queen, Prince of Wales; Queen of Spain; Queen of Norway; Crown Princess of Sweden; Sultan of Johore, and "two hundred other titled English men and English Women."

3,000 people hear Pianola at Conservatory of Moscow: "The appearance of an automatic instrument, playing with a great orchestra, was amazing to the Russians."

Jack London takes Victor talking machine to South Seas, where it's a hit.

In England, for a penny in pubs, great automatic band-pianos, with drum, cymbal, mandolin, violin, and glass panel with electric lights behind which cause to appear on panel live volcanoes, waterfalls, &c., called moving pictures.

McTammany: "I was doing a good business making money hand over fist and having a bully good time. . . ."

1909

370,000 pianos built; 35,000 players; grand holding at its 1904 level of 7,000.

The Story of Dance Music by Henry W. Hart done by the Autopiano Company, who say, "The Autopiano is the piano upon which *anyone* can play, *any music*, at once without previous training of any kind."

Their piano praised by: His Holiness Pope Pius X̣, the Sultan of Turkey, Alexander Graham Bell, the Wright Bros., Prince Tadashigo Shimedsu—and installed on 32 battleships.

"John D. Rockfeller, Andrew Carnegie, William Howard Taft, and other public figures played golf for diversion, for exercise, and, frequently for the correction of digestive ailments. President Taft's love for the links was intense and it was said that, with the single exception of the Philippines, 'there is no subject which the President likes better to discuss than golf and its possibilities as a popular pastime.' " (*New York Daily Tribune* editorial, Oct. 10, **1909**)

The roll was marked along its route with instructions, not to be confused with genuine musical directions (signature and time) and for a creditable performance the operator was obliged to watch for such apocryphal warnings as PP and Largo, and for sudden liberties like Presto.

1910

Total piano output 360,000, no monopoly (Aeolian & American made less than one-tenth); others centered round Chicago incl. Rudolph Wurlitzer of Cincinnati.

By this time Wurlitzer had devised an automatic harp, whose strings were plucked by tiny automatic fingers; also responsible for the Monster Military Band Organ, the Mandolin Quartette, the PianOrchestra, and a $500 gimmick called the Pianino.

Mrs. Eddy dies. C.S. destroy plates of her biography.

Robber barons had used $ to fight; now emerge in new character of philanthropists, foundations.

Boy Scouts formed.

Tolstoy dies.

E. Glyn returning from Russia, train to Warsaw and kidnapping attempt in Poland, which confirmed suspicion that the Russian czar "had spoken of *Three Weeks* as being a book about his wife; she remembered the American's tale about the Czarina; and she came to the conclusion that the plot against her life had been hatched in Tsarskoe Selo and that her enemy was someone in the Imperial entourage."

Decade **1900–10**, rate of pianos increases 6.2 times that of human beings.

Walter J. Travis: "Many men . . . ignoring the ridicule which surely would have been their portion a couple of years ago, they have consoled themselves with the reflection that what is good enough for the President is good enough for them."

1911

Revue Musicale de Paris (trans.): At the opening of the piece, no 3/4, nor 6/8 nor 9/12; in what follows, no separation of one measure from another; no evaluated silences for a pause or a breath; nothing which informs one of a syncopation or an anticipation; the notes which follow and resemble one another leave the performer the care of disembroiling the rhythm, if it is possible, and plunging him, from the beginning, into uncertainty, trouble, and hesitation.

Hollerith sold out to Int'l Machine Corp.

1912

Dale Carnegie begins giving courses (N.Y.): How to Win Friends. . . .

U.S. triumph at Olympic Games Stockholm: *Blackwood's Magazine* typified British hostility to overspecialized athletics by contending that the United States contingent was "run on business lines" and that America's victory was attained neither through American athletic superiority nor British decadence, but through professionalism alone: "And it is precisely this spirit of professionalism, this lust to win, which we hope will never be introduced into Great Britain. Wherever professionalism has flourished there has been an end of sport."

McTammany, concerning those who snubbed him because they were making money, &c.: "Those men have traveled part of the way, are ascending the eastern declivity of life. Some day, like me, they will be descending the western side. Then it will be different."

Letter, while he is deathly sick at Noroton (headed "From the Common People"): from A. W. Glick, Kennewick, Wash.: "I hope you may fully recover. You can at least truthfully say that you have lived for some purpose."

History of the Player by John McTammany:
> The writing: ". . . with one hand I held the grim monster at bay, while with the other I traced the tortuous pathway of the player."
> The opening: "Marvel not, therefore, if I carry the reader back to the scenes and incidents of the Civil War, the times of our ancestors. . . ."

1913

J. P. Morgan dies.

Santayana: "For utility makes beauty, & eyes bulging out from the head like his are the most advantageous for seeing; nostrils wide & open to the air, like his, most appropriate for smell; & a mouth large & voluminous, like his, best fitted for both eating & kissing."

On Walt Whitman and the "charm of uniformity in multiplicity": "Everywhere it greets us with a passionate preference; not flowers but leaves of grass, not music but drum-taps, not composition but aggregation, not the hero but the average man, not the crisis but the vulgarest moment; & by this resolute marshalling of nullities, by this effort to show us everything as a momentary pulsation of a liquid & structureless whole, he profoundly stirs the imagination."

As for the ultimate consumer of all this musical feast, the American music lover, he ate it up and cried for more. No longer did he have to exert himself even to the extent of pumping pedals or pushing levers. An electric motor now reduced his chores to zero. He merely sat back, relaxed, and dreamed, while his piano, entirely on its own, delivered performances by the giants of the keyboard, from Pachmann and Godowsky to Vincent Lopez, right in his own living room. No czar, sultan, or begum could command more. [clipping]

1914

325,000 pianos built: 235,000 uprights; 10,000 grands; 80,000 players.

More money spent in this industry on litigations than probably any other in such a space of time.

> chewing gum
> aluminum household utensils
> airplanes and seaplanes
>   [clipping]

William Dean Howells, somewhat shaken by the U.S. he saw (he'd been a most optimistic type), now felt it was the office of the American writer, better & kinder, to write books concerned with the dawning movement of social justice; tried to reaffirm faith in U.S. middle-class values, but by 1915 "my sort of fiction is no longer desired."

Sarah Norcliffe (check name):
>The golf links lie so near the mill that almost every day
>The laboring children can look out and watch the men at play.

The Music Trade Review, vol. 61, no. 9, whole issue: "Every player on the market now will play anything with perfect correctness, perfect time. But it has become now a 'true musical instrument.' "

Article leaves future of the film theatre up to automatic players for music to harmonize with character of films presented. Film dramatist is limited: ". . . he cannot show any character development; he cannot work far ahead of his audience; he cannot work with any but the most primitive emotions, and he cannot interpret . . . and it is just here that music steps in."

Jack London wrote for money, hopes to make his books serve social purpose, hasten social revolution in U.S., crusades for social justice; dies (1916), probably a suicide, age 40; owned baronial estate resembling medieval castle; 41 books in 14 years: disillusioned.

John Reed's reaction to the Roosevelt nomination at the Progressive Party convention in Chicago: "he is back with the people among whom alone he is comfortable, 'the predatory plutocrats.' At least he is no longer tied to democracy. For that he undoubtedly breathes a sigh of relief. And as for democracy, we can only hope that some day it will cease to put its trust in men."

Niall Brennan, *The Making of a Moron*, Sheed & Ward, 1953: "In 1917 . . . the New York state textile factories had been short of labour. There was a state of war, business was brisk, but manpower was precious. The Utica Knitting Mill made an arrangement with the Rome Institution for

Mentally defective Girls . . . twenty-four girls whose mental ages ranged from six to ten years . . . were put to work at the mill." Happy surprise at results: girls kept on after war emergency: behaviour better, more punctual, more regular in their habits, and they do "not indulge in as much 'gossip and levity.' "

Immigration literacy test instituted (till now anyone was welcome, illiterate or not, as cheap labor).

E. Glyn arrangements to write for American press, permits to visit battlefields came through, she to Paris: "What has happened to the gallant French nation that I used to adore? So much of the aristocracy here in Paris seems to be just *fin de race*. The little shop-keepers near the lines are carrying on their business with unruffled calm, but the real source of their contentment is not patriotism but merely greed. . . ."

(Later) "The women have a sex urge but they are vicious with over-civilization. . . . among the lay population, to those who have lost no loved ones and have suffered no decrease of wealth, the war is simply a *bore.* . . ."

(Paris) "One young widow was there tonight, her husband only killed four weeks ago, so bored, she said, with the funeral ceremonies and her mother-in-law's crocodile tears, that she had to come out and dance for a little! She was wrapped in a yard or so of black chiffon and apparently nothing else. . . ."

1919

Players outnumbered straight pianos, were 53 percent of industry output: 341,652 total.

Radios: **1920**, 5,000; **1924**, 2.5 million.

Describe postwar emancipation of women as related to "accomplishments" of previous generation, i.e., piano; also, and part of, devaluation of home as significant center of living.

The Pianola as a Means of Personal Expression by Alvin Landon Coburn (**1920**). He holds that it is an instrument for the artist; taking 2 hrs. practice a day for a year to master it. Its deadliest enemy the mediocre pianist. Different from gramophone whose records are invariable performances.

Outside player's fingers drop ½ inch; advantage that keys were struck from the front, as with the human hand, whereas the inside players, up until 1906, gave less satisfactory tones because the keys were depressed from the back.

". . . the arts must accept the new conditions and make the most of them."

Lasky had got to Hollywood to combat hostility of dramatic critics and litterateurs toward movies. Maeterlinck, Smrset Maugham, Gertrude Atherton, and E. Glyn arrived there in **1920**.

"It did not take the authors long to discover that their presence in Hollywood was only windowdressing." (E.G. is 56 in 1920?)

E. Glyn of R. Valentino: "Do you know he had never even thought of kissing the palm, rather than the back, of a woman's hand until I made him do it!"

Dame Nellie Melba sang over radio at Chelmsford, Eng., heard in Persia.

Reed as communist leader was indicted in absentia, in Russia in fact, where, though he tried to get home, died age 33 of typhus, lay in state for a week in Moscow's trade union center, at all odds the only *Lampoon* man to be buried in Kremlin wall.

The De-Assification of Music by C. B. Chilton, of the Intrinsic Music Foundation, Tomkins Square, N.Y.C. (**1922**). Quotes Dumaurier, Peter Ibbetson's despair, calling him an "antedeluvian or prehistoric musician who cannot play and is therefore shut out of the delights of music." Here: "Next I would buy or beg or borrow the music that had filled me with such emotion and delight, and take it home to my little square piano, and try to finger it out for myself. But I had begun too late in life. . . . to sit, longing and helpless, before an instrument one cannot play, with a lovely score one cannot read!"

All of this work toward music education (citing the shortage of music teachers, voice teachers, music appreciation in the Midwest, &c., &c.). Chilton sees the player as going out, and only he can save it; also only it can save music: as the coming of the printed page was to the novel, so is his invention to music education.

Isadora Duncan, who'd done much to liberate art, invited to Moscow by Soviet Union to set up a school; got lover Sergei Essenine, poet of the proles, coarse, alcoholic, brawling: married & exported him from Russia; E.'s poetic creed: "Let us be Asiatics. Let us smell evilly! Let us shamelessly scratch our backsides in front of everybody." Daily scenes, when they arrived in U.S. high anti-Soviet feeling; they are detained at Ellis Island as political agents, hounded by police during her disastrous U.S. tour; she finally returned to Russia, shed her beatnik, wandered Europe, died (Nice, **1927**) with scarf—car wheels.

1923

350,000 pianos built; by **1932**, 30,000; **1941**, 161,000.

Fisher Body kilties bagpipe band.

MGM does "3 Weeks." E. Glyn script, Aileen Pringle & Conrad Nagel. Mrs. Glyn at about age 56? 59? Instructing Aileen in scene lying "on the tiger skin, quivering with emotion and passion."

Published *The Philosophy of Love*, and gave 10 minute talks on love in N.Y. vaudeville at $500 a week.

1924

Judge calls U.S. "idealistic, spiritual" nation in banning Schnitzler's Cassanova books.

Petrillo has been making radio stations pay musicians: house bombed.

1925

Indiana Standard Oil mandolin club formed.

Total piano output 306,584 (down 10 percent from 1919; population up 8 percent).

Music and Letters (a London quarterly): "The player-Piano" by Sidney Grew (also in this issue: advertisement for Columbia Grafonola).

Grieg and Padereweski approved the player around the beginning of the century, by playing rolls for it. . . . Many musicians recognized it as an art medium, but dealers did not care to have it known that any skill was involved or required, or study. However, the Aeolian Company recognized its art, and sold it as such. Compton Mackenzie is quoted as saying that taking up the player made him more exacting in his music appreciation, but he sees it as rather a refinement, too exacting. (He had a Bluther-Carola in 1924.)

The more that music played departs from the "banjo beat" (Liszt, Chaminade, Moszkowski) to the more complex and involved rhythms and changing times (Debussy, Ravel) the more the instrument played as "automatic" distorts it.

Mrs. Curwen (?who she?) found herself "horribly at the mercy of the demon"—she couldn't control it.

From **1910–25** it remained the same instrument, with few devices added.

Concert use awkward because, perhaps in the middle of a sonata movement, must pause, rewind, and insert new roll. (Suggests two pianos, and artist may move from one to other on stage.) But it is realized that no such person will ever be regarded or respected as an artist, a virtuoso—still called by the ignorant an operator.

Liszt as almost self-playing, Brahms at times almost impossible.

Essenine's suicide.

"Complacency": the condition from which and the condition to which behavior is always in process of moving.

1927

AFL's Green tells musicians they differ from other manual workers.

Petrillo gains control of turntable operators for radio in Chicago.

Music given high trade rank at Detroit trade school.

Glendale, Calif., mayor: city w/out music is a graveyard.

Kafka's *America* published Munich.

British psychologist labels Thorndike anarchic, in argument on testing theories.

1928

22,300 movie houses, 834 releases.

Total 62 strikes.

E. Glyn staying with Marion Davies beach house, Hollywood.

1929

FoxMovietone pleads free speech with first talking films.

Glyn to England for a visit, stayed there the rest of her life, where she returned "under strong influence of spiritualism and the occult . . .": séances to reach dead friends.

Dabbled in automatic writing (which she'd first experimented with in Egypt, 1920, wrote several pages of faultless Arabic of which she knew not a word).

Out of E.G.'s first 14 novels the heroes of 12 have no peacetime occupation at all.

Sousa induced to conduct on radio.

Anecdotes referencing stimulating-work property of music, women washing floor, morale, testimonials, getting business, pep, prospect of enlarged leisure, rhythm of work: cow yields milk to music, girls make more underwear.

Man's mind differs from lower forms in no. of connections, no qualitative but quantitative difference; search for physiological cause of intellect; intelligence as number of connections a man has, i.e., describing not a mind but a computer.

For 20 years the industry had been advertising, Why play the piano with your hands when you can pump it with your feet and hear the artist? In those years, a whole generation grew up which took them at their words and could not play with their hands. Consequently sales figures above, and the radio in **1926** which was recognized as a threat. The industry formed a committee that year to go about country to school supervisors asking to have piano lessons given at 25¢ apiece. In Chicago, 12,000 children, in other cities 3–5,000 average, took advantage of it. Since the player piano had been wheeled into the corner in 1926 and no one could play the piano. Then: in **1935** the trade changed the styling of pianos to the spinet, which found favor; meanwhile the children, having grown up, who had taken lessons, were learning to appreciate and being inspired to want to make piano music themselves by the radio.

Today the industry is constantly being bothered by inventors who present themselves with new "featherweight" player actions, &c., the manufacturers know that if they started it again, the new generation which has grown up without players would go off their rockers with delight, as they did in 1912, but they are wiser after the way they paid for going on with their fad to such a degree that they came close to killing the whole piano industry.

INDEX

abortion, 103, 112

Absalom, Absalom! (Faulkner), 136

Abscam, 60

absolutism, 92–93

Acheson, Dean, 51

Adam and Eve, 100

Adventures of Augie March (Bellow), 73

Adventures of Huckleberry Finn, The (Twain), 55

Aeolian, 3

"Agapē Agape: The Secret History of the Player Piano," x, 6–13, 15
  commentary on, 6–7
  text, 7–13

Agapē Agape (Gaddis), viii, xiii, xix, 141
  summary notes on the work in progress, 141–45

Albany Times Union, 110

Alger, Horatio, 10–11

Allen, Woody, 42

Alvarez, A., 38

American Academy of Arts, 132

Ampico, 3

Animal Intelligence (Thorndike), 9

aporia, xiii, xiv, xvi, 99, 134

Aristotle, 90

Armageddon, 100

Armstrong, Karen, 101

Arto-roll, 4

Ashcroft, John, 80, 86

Assemblies of God, 103

Atlantic Monthly, 1, 141

Augustine, St., 89

automation, 49

B-1 bomber, 67–68

B-2 bomber, 117

Babbitt (character), 44–45, 47, 52, 53

Baptists, 101

Barnes, Julian, 128

Barth, John, 136

Barthes, Roland, 97

Bell, Daniel, 54–55

Bellamy, Edward, 38, 41–42

Bellow, Saul, vii, 136
  Gaddis's review of *More Die of Heartbreak,* vii, 72–79

Benjamin, Walter, xvii–xviii, 137, 145

Bennett, William J., 86

Bernhardt, Madame, 10

Biff Loman (character), 54, 55–56

birth control, 96, 103

Boccaccio, Giovanni, 94, 95

FOR THE BEST IN PAPERBACKS, LOOK FOR THE

In every corner of the world, on every subject under the sun, Penguin represents quality and variety—the very best in publishing today.

For complete information about books available from Penguin—including Puffins, Penguin Classics, and Compass—and how to order them, write to us at the appropriate address below. Please note that for copyright reasons the selection of books varies from country to country.

In the United Kingdom: Please write to *Dept. EP, Penguin Books Ltd, Bath Road, Harmondsworth, West Drayton, Middlesex UB7 0DA.*

In the United States: Please write to *Penguin Putnam Inc., P.O. Box 12289 Dept. B, Newark, New Jersey 07101-5289* or call 1-800-788-6262.

In Canada: Please write to *Penguin Books Canada Ltd, 10 Alcorn Avenue, Suite 300, Toronto, Ontario M4V 3B2.*

In Australia: Please write to *Penguin Books Australia Ltd, P.O. Box 257, Ringwood, Victoria 3134.*

In New Zealand: Please write to *Penguin Books (NZ) Ltd, Private Bag 102902, North Shore Mail Centre, Auckland 10.*

In India: Please write to *Penguin Books India Pvt Ltd, 11 Panchsheel Shopping Centre, Panchsheel Park, New Delhi 110 017.*

In the Netherlands: Please write to *Penguin Books Netherlands bv, Postbus 3507, NL-1001 AH Amsterdam.*

In Germany: Please write to *Penguin Books Deutschland GmbH, Metzlerstrasse 26, 60594 Frankfurt am Main.*

In Spain: Please write to *Penguin Books S. A., Bravo Murillo 19, 1° B, 28015 Madrid.*

In Italy: Please write to *Penguin Italia s.r.l., Via Benedetto Croce 2, 20094 Corsico, Milano.*

In France: Please write to *Penguin France, Le Carré Wilson, 62 rue Benjamin Baillaud, 31500 Toulouse.*

In Japan: Please write to *Penguin Books Japan Ltd, Kaneko Building, 2-3-25 Koraku, Bunkyo-Ku, Tokyo 112.*

In South Africa: Please write to *Penguin Books South Africa (Pty) Ltd, Private Bag X14, Parkview, 2122 Johannesburg.*

Printed in the United States
by Baker & Taylor Publisher Services